**CCCC STUDIES IN WRITING & RHETORIC**
*Edited by Steve Parks, University of Virginia*

The aim of the CCCC Studies in Writing & Rhetoric (SWR) Series is to influence how we think about language in action and especially how writing gets taught at the college level. The methods of studies vary from the critical to historical to linguistic to ethnographic, and their authors draw on work in various fields that inform composition—including rhetoric, communication, education, discourse analysis, psychology, cultural studies, and literature. Their focuses are similarly diverse—ranging from individual writers and teachers, to work on classrooms and communities and curricula, to analyses of the social, political, and material contexts of writing and its teaching.

SWR was one of the first scholarly book series to focus on the teaching of writing. It was established in 1980 by the Conference on College Composition and Communication (CCCC) in order to promote research in the emerging field of writing studies. As our field has grown, the research sponsored by SWR has continued to articulate the commitment of CCCC to supporting the work of writing teachers as reflective practitioners and intellectuals.

We are eager to identify influential work in writing and rhetoric as it emerges. We thus ask authors to send us project proposals that clearly situate their work in the field and show how they aim to redirect our ongoing conversations about writing and its teaching. Proposals should include an overview of the project, a brief annotated table of contents, and a sample chapter. They should not exceed 10,000 words.

To submit a proposal, please register as an author at www.editorialmanager.com/nctebp. Once registered, follow the steps to submit a proposal (be sure to choose SWR Book Proposal from the drop-down list of article submission types).

# Transnational Assemblages

## Social Justice and Crisis Communication during Disaster

Sweta Baniya

*Virginia Polytechnic Institute and State University*

Conference on College Composition and Communication

National Council of Teachers of English

www.ncte.org

The WAC Clearinghouse

wac.colostate.edu

Staff Editor: Kurt Austin
Manuscript Editor: Meg Vezzu
Series Editor: Steve Parks
Interior Design: Mary Rohrer
Layout: Mike Palmquist
Cover Design: Pat Mayer
Cover Image: Kishor Sharma
Cover Image Caption: Women building a memorial to mark one-year anniversary of the 2015 Nepal earthquake in Barpark, Gorkha, the epicenter of the Nepal earthquake.

Print ISBN: 978-0-8141-0193-3; epub ISBN: 978-0-8141-0194-0; PDF ISBN: 978-0-8141-0195-7



This book is copublished with the WAC Clearinghouse. It is available in open-access digital formats at wac.colostate.edu.

**Library of Congress Cataloging-in-Publication Data**

A catalog record of this book has been requested.

**CONTENTS**

To disaster responders, who remind us of courage, wisdom, and selflessness in the darkest hours, and to two fierce women in my life: my Ama, Gyanu Pandey Baniya, and my Dijju Him Kumari Baniya, for being the force behind me.

# Acknowledgments

I am grateful to my husband, Dr. Carlos Pérez-Torres, my father, Gokul Baniya, my brother, Bishesh Baniya, and my sister-in-law, Nilima Shrestha. I am grateful to my own transnational assemblages of mentors, friends, students, colleagues, and communities both online and offline in Nepal, Puerto Rico, Blacksburg, Virginia, and beyond borders. You all know who you are! I can't be grateful enough for kindness, love, and mentorship that you all provide. It is with all your love, support, and mentorship, this project has been possible.

Thank you to dear friend Kishor K. Sharma for providing a powerful picture for the cover. Thank you, Department of English, Virginia Tech, and Dean of the College of Liberal Arts and Human Sciences,Dr. Laura Belmonte for providing subvention funds to make this book open access. Thank you, Dr. Steve Parks, Dr. Stephanie Kerschbaum, and the NCTE team for everything you have done for this book. This book has been possible due to grants that I have received from Center for Intercultural Learning, Mentorship, Assessment, and Research (CILMAR) at Purdue University that funded my travel to Nepal and from the Center for Puerto Rican Studies, where the then-chair Dr. Edwin Meléndez with one email of inquiry provided funds to go to Puerto Rico. Thank you, Sonia Deana, for careful copy edits of my book proposal, chapters, and book.

Lastly, the participants of my research who trusted me with their stories to tell it to the world. Without you all, this book wouldn't be possible.

# Foreword

That moment I knew I had to study how people communicate during times of disaster. It hit me like a ton of bricks, knowing I had to do something, understand the phenomenon, collect that data, and eventually share whatever knowledge surfaces. That need to connect, to support, to help, to learn, to share. The decisions we make to build these careers and spend our lives learning from others and aiming to show our societies ways to move forward more productively, that is the stuff of technical communication.

So back to that moment. It was the photo of a missing child posted to Flickr, a boy the same age as my now 22-year-old daughter, that spurred me on to studying how people communicate in these moments of crisis. Ripped from the arms of his mother during a tsunami, the post about him became the center of my world as I set out to understand how people were coordinating across time and space to reunite him with his family. How did a Flickr post become the central hub for coordinating information? Twenty years ago, Flickr was a popular photo sharing website, not a site set up to manage posts about missing persons. How did this intersect with translation across Red Cross and Red Crescent sites? Participants, mostly women, repeatedly searched other websites for clues, reporting back on the Flickr post. How could we design these user experiences to make this work easier, faster, more efficient? And, to quote my dissertation co-chair Dr. June Deery, "why are we only hearing about the white people?"

The ways in which we break barriers in society and especially academia is often a slow, plodding, excruciating exercise. My weaksauce answer to June was "well, that's who is using Flickr," and while definitely ham-fisted, it speaks to that digital, political, social, and economic divide. As Dr. Allegra Smith stated to me so eloquently, the whiteness of Flickr in the midst of a decidedly nonwhite disaster zone speaks to the need for intersectional analyses of the coordination of information in times of crisis. What Dr. Sweta Baniya has done with this book is to walk through this next step. While I can easily write about my own experiences during disasters, I cannot do what Sweta has done here, through her transnational and local lens, her understanding of her own time and place. That space we make to step forward, the space all of us must build, nurture, respect, and get out of the way of is critical to our understanding as rhetoricians, technical communicators, scholars, and people sharing this small blue planet of ours.

It helps me to recall this quote from Carl Sagan, one that helps me guide my work: "Our planet is a lonely speck in the great enveloping cosmic dark. In our obscurity, in all this vastness, there is no hint that help will come from elsewhere to save us from ourselves." And there it is—the reason why we study how people coordinate, communicate, and survive in the worst possible moments any of us could experience.

There is something particularly special for me in writing this foreword for Sweta, knowing that this work will continue. When Hurricane Maria slammed into the awesome island where my grandmother was born, my only thoughts were about the safety of my cousins, aunts, and uncles. As my mother and I tried to check in on them, I recalled so many other massive storms I had lived through while growing up in south Florida. Something I am certain that Sweta herself felt even more pressing, having to experience the earthquake in Nepal at a distance. That pale blue dot, that vastness, and that need to help each other.

It continues to be an honor to support Sweta's research, to watch her launch this book into a universe that desperately needs all of us working toward the goal of minimizing the impact of disasters on our most vulnerable populations. I have no doubt that Sweta has a lifetime of work ahead of her because of our never-ending wars, famines, and climate change. And now we have the gift of her book, one that will create space for further research and teaching about marginalized spaces.

Thank you for doing this work, Sweta. And thank you to everyone who comes after Sweta to continue this work. We must walk humbly as scholars, communicators, and people if we are to help build the world we hope to live in.

– Liza Potts, PhD, Michigan State University

# Preamble: April 25, 2015

It was a normal Saturday afternoon in Kathmandu, the capital city of Nepal. All schools, colleges, and government offices were closed, but most businesses, shops, and restaurants were open as usual. I was attending a conference, the International Folklore Congress, where people from different parts of the world gathered. Around 11:40 a.m. local time, I was taking selfies, tweeting, and texting as I prepared to attend a presentation about urbanization. The room was filled with 30-40 individuals. Suddenly, the building started to shake violently. I went into shock and was disoriented, but I remember that all the people in the room began to rush toward the door, screaming and fighting against the shaking building, not knowing what to do next. I asked someone, "Is this an earthquake?" to which they replied, "No." I ran under a table, thinking it would keep me safe. As I write this, years later, I can still feel myself trembling in that instant.

Within a few moments, though, I, along with the others, ran out of the building. Fortunately, the conference building was one of the lucky edifices that hadn't collapsed. After reaching a safe spot, I checked Twitter on my phone. Within five minutes of the chaos, pictures, news articles, and information began to circulate worldwide, informing everyone that a 7.5 magnitude earthquake had struck Nepal. It was hard for me to comprehend what I had just faced. All the people in that room along with my family and close friends had survived, but more than 8,000 people lost their lives, and around 26,000 were injured throughout the 14 districts of Nepal on that day.

In 2015, I had two jobs and an online presence in Nepal. I worked as an English newsreader at Radio Nepal, Nepal's national radio station, and I worked as a communications officer at a nonprofit organization called Teach for Nepal. Both jobs and my online presence made me a disaster responder as a journalist and a communications practitioner managing community-based disaster response. Following the earthquake, I was immediately reporting, tweeting, replying, and retweeting, as were thousands of Nepalis in Nepal and abroad and non-Nepalis. Nepal is considered one of the most vulnerable populations during a time of disaster, but after the earthquake, I witnessed the rhetorical agency of the Nepalis in responding to a disaster and managing the aftermath. As a responder to the Nepal earthquake, I witnessed discrepancies in aid distribution and crisis communication that exacerbated social injustices.

Disillusionment made me pursue a PhD in rhetoric and composition. Experiences during other crises in both Nepal and the US motivated me to explore how systems of oppression aggravate the consequences of disasters among the most vulnerable and marginalized communities; how technology, which is crucial for the survival of such communities, creates dire circumstances by reinforcing inequities; and how marginalized communities use and create technology for their survival and resistance.

Admiration of the power of the vulnerable and marginalized to resist their own oppression led to my writing this book.

# Introduction

Disasters are uncertain, yet inevitable.

Disasters impact marginalized communities disproportionately, yet this does not need to be inevitable.

We need to rethink the scholarship and practices related to disasters.

Currently, disaster scholars call for stronger crisis preparation, investment in community resilience, and the development of technological and communication infrastructures. I intend to expand this disciplinary call by focusing on global crises and their effects on marginalized communities. I hope to disrupt deeply rooted inequalities that create severe imbalances in communication and aid distribution during a disaster to those most in need. To this end, I argue for the need to integrate the knowledge and the lived experiences of marginalized community members into the collective goal of social change. I demonstrate how transnational knowledge-making and community-based practices by these very communities tackle social injustices in the wake of global disasters. I demonstrate how locals in marginalized and colonized spaces like Nepal and Puerto Rico respectively overcome the complexities created by disasters through transnational coalitional engagements. To draw out the value of their insights, I expand the boundaries of traditional assemblage theory through a framework infused with theories of social justice and intersectionality. This new theoretical framework highlights how locals in marginalized and colonized spaces overcome disaster-created complexities via coalitional and transnational engagements. Ultimately, I argue that during a disaster, technical communicators can play a crucial role in creating a network that deconstructs the complex networks of communication with critical approaches and a social justice-oriented framework. Such a framework will highlight, recognize, and value the actions of marginalized communities in the face of catastrophic disasters (Jones et al.).

### DISASTERS AS GLOBAL CONCERNS WITH LOCAL INTERVENTIONS

A disaster shifts geography, people, and culture. It also initiates movement in space, causes various networks to form, and creates a local space for global stakeholders to act. Different types of networked communications begin to occur. Daniel Aldrich defines a disaster as "an event that suspends normal activities and threatens or causes severe, communitywide damage" (3). Indeed, larger-scale crises create disruptions in normalcy by causing threats to living entities' well-being and natural or infrastructural damages. The United Nations Office of Disaster Risk Reduction (UNDRR) defines a disaster as "a serious disruption of the functioning of a community or a society at any scale due to hazardous events interacting with conditions of exposure, vulnerability and capacity, leading to one or more of the following: human, material, economic and environmental losses and impacts" ("Disaster"). Therefore, disasters are events that have extreme, large-scale impacts that affect a great number of lives. They can have a multidimensional effect that requires the involvement of national, local and international entities to address the aftermath. So, disasters disrupt people's normal lives, but they also bring local people together to form various communities both in online and offline spaces via public discourses on the web, collective interactions in transcultural ways, and through the sharing of the affective sentiment (Ding; Papacharissi; Baniya "The Implications of"). As such, the discourses of local catastrophic disasters transcend boundaries as these disasters become a global concern.

The sharing of data, information, and resources needed to address the consequences of a disaster also helps in the formation of a transnational discourse. Catastrophic events create multidisciplinary networked participatory actions within the local and global communities such that the global community participates by responding to the local disasters (Aldrich et al.; Kim and Hastak; Murthy and Gross; Baniya "Transnational Assemblages"). Such networked actions (Castells) have been made possible with the advances in information and communication technologies that use social networking to make information more accessible (Toya and Skidmore). Going back to the history, technical communication was used in the context of World War II to explain about weapon operations (Connors). However, in the current context where technologies have advanced, we are living in a golden age for technical and professional communication where worldwide there is more engagement in these platforms than ever (Kimball). Digital technologies and resources make the local discourse on disaster reach global communities in a faster, easier, and more effective way.

People around the globe can engage with the discourse of the victims of local disasters, thus providing those actors with platforms and communities with whom they can collaborate and take action to address their immediate needs.

While disasters are uncertain, currently, inequities in response seem to be inevitable. Such injustices result in the loss of lives, displacement, and permanent damage to the most vulnerable of populations. These inequities will continue unless we take steps to change the way we understand and approach a crisis. Take Nepal and Puerto Rico. These two culturally, geographically, and contextually different locations confronted surprisingly similar battles in the aftermath of the disasters. Recorded as one of the biggest disasters in nearly a century, the Nepal earthquake created chaos in 14 districts by taking the lives of 8,979 people, injuring 26,000, and sparking a humanitarian crisis. The disaster added to the burden of existing social, political, and climate-related crises in Nepal, which is still recovering from the ten-year-long civil war (1996–2006) manifested in its current political instability. Due to climate change, millions of rural, marginalized, and vulnerable Nepalis also suffer from problems such as reductions in agricultural production, food insecurity, strained water resources, loss of forests and biodiversity, and damaged infrastructure (*Climate Risk Profile: Nepal*). The earthquake put the already vulnerable Nepalis at risk, resulting in the rise of poverty, human trafficking, and debt (Chandran). Due to a lack of understanding of community needs, difficulty in communication and logistics, as well as a centralized approach to disaster response during the earthquake, many rural communities did not receive the support they needed (Hall et al.). These discrepancies were challenged by local grassroots activists and disaster responders who, using digital media, invited the global community to stand in solidarity and help the suffering Nepalis by sending unprecedented volumes of technical, financial, and humanitarian aid (Government of Nepal, 4). Yet these voices are not part of our research or seen as part of the solution to such disasters.

Hurricane Maria devastated Puerto Rico along with several other Caribbean islands, causing an estimated $90 billion in damages, making it the third costliest tropical cyclone in the United States since 1900 (Kishore et al. 163). Initially, the official death count in Puerto Rico was only 64. A report by Nishant Kishore et al. claimed that the death toll exceeded 4,645, which is 70 times more than the official estimate.

Much like the Nepal earthquake, Hurricane Maria exacerbated the vulnerability of Puerto Rican communities who are suffering through "an ongoing recession, insurmountable debt, and coloniality" (Soto Vega). The lack of electric power and mobile phone networks after the hurricane caused a serious communication crisis which cut the island off from the rest of the world. The hurricane, as Hilda Lloréns argues, also brought endemic risks, vulnerabilities, and hidden crises into view, affecting the infirm, the disabled, those without access to transportation, those living in isolated areas, and those living in extreme poverty (159). The hurricane also brought to light the ongoing sovereignty struggles and how colonialism, the severity of protocols, and negligence by the US government impacted the most vulnerable. Here again, many local disaster responders and grassroots activists both on the island and the mainland (the Puerto Rican diaspora) launched a decentralized disaster response effort informed by decolonial practices (Cortés; Lloréns; Soto Vega). These actors need to inform our research as they play a larger part in the solution.

My experiences from the Nepal earthquake were still fresh in my mind while I observed the devastation created by Hurricane Maria in Puerto Rico. I recognized comparable aid distribution complications, and I understood and emphasized the communities who resisted and overcame the consequences of the catastrophe and political incompetence at the same time. Moreover, Nepal is a country that is facing many of the consequences of climate change and is often prone to compounding crises including political unrest, such as a ten-year-long civil war that killed thousands, and years of political instability. The earthquake further embattled the country and stalled the nation's development by pushing an additional 700,000–982,000 people below the poverty line (Sapkota). Likewise, in Puerto Rico, the colonial consequences led to a lack of support and negligence by the United States. The consequences of Hurricane Maria in Puerto Rico unraveled ongoing sovereignty struggles and pushed activists toward grassroots, decolonial practices (Cortés; Lloréns; Soto Vega, "Colonial Causes and Consequences"). Additionally, the demographics of each country have very specific identity markers that make people more vulnerable and marginalized based on their race, class, gender, sexuality, and, in the case of Nepal, caste. In both Nepal and Puerto Rico, the failure of systems and governmental mechanisms caused the suffering of vulnerable communities and led to the emergence of local activists to support such troubled communities by developing survival praxis with global reach. The disasters, therefore, brought the world together to network, participate, and act and help in the emergence of transnational networked communities in Nepal and Puerto Rico (Frost; Potts; Baniya "Transnational Assemblages"). These communities, both online and offline, worked together to build their knowledge about each disaster by developing unique composition and communication practices. Such practices helped the Nepali and Puerto Rican communities in disseminating information, drawing the attention of stakeholders, raising funds, and performing relief and rescue operations. Because of this realization, I have chosen to put the Nepal earthquake and Hurricane Maria side by side when analyzing the aftermath of a calamity. My hope is to bring these voices to our field and into disaster response practices.

I believe these activists' rhetorical practices should inform our field as it prepares scholars, students, and practitioners to work during any kind of future disaster. I hope to expand upon the rhetorical discourses on global disasters by creating a space that brings the experiences of people from marginalized communities to the forefront. And I hope my comparative study of the Nepal and Puerto Rico disasters, contexts, and cultures presents a nuanced representation of these rhetorical practices by providing a grounding for understanding similarities and differences in multiple marginalized contexts. As such, I argue for the inclusion of the voices of people who have been overlooked by current scholarship, because their actions and communication practices enrichen our understanding of disaster rhetoric. And I am not alone in this call. Rhetoric and technical and professional communication (TPC) scholars have long recognized that uncertainty plays a key role in the deliberation over risks, and these scholars urge communicators to adopt a consistent rhetorical framework for navigating uncertainty. Over the years, disaster scholarship has focused on industrial disasters, environmental disasters, war, bomb blasts, shootings, oil spills, epidemics, and climate change (Angeli; Ding *Rhetoric*; Frost; Lee; Potts, "Designing for Disaster"; Sauer; Richards; Walwema; Grace and Tham; Powell; Hawhee; Clark; Welhausen). Recently, however, the focus on disasters within the United States and beyond has expanded and shifted toward studying the importance of a) writing, information design, and delivery; b) networked communities and digital actions; and c) transnational work, including global grassroots movements, issues of climate change, and human rights (Dingo; Hesford and Schell; Kynard; Parks and Hachelaf; Schell; Sackey; Simmons). Given this shift in focus, Huiling Ding believes that there is a need for a "transcultural risk analysis model that [features] transcultural forces, global flows, power dynamics, knowledge production and negotiations and impacts of local contexts on risk communication practices" (240, *Rhetoric*).

While disaster issues concern scholars, we need studies that incorporate both qualitative and quantitative research to develop a model that better frames the rhetorical situation of global disasters. We need to expand the disaster rhetoric such that it incorporates social justice theories to recognize how local populations use technology to create oppositional global rhetoric in the aftermath of a disaster. Such a framework needs grounding that is easily adaptable and can be contextualized to understand the counter models of disaster response, aid distribution, and the community's perspective. Angela Haas and Michelle Eble argue that globalization affects three critical spheres of technical communication's influence—technological, scientific, and cultural—and in highly complex ways. Hence, as various disasters continue to rattle the world, TPC scholars must develop newer and innovative studies that showcase how activism from marginalized communities can help in shaping writing and communication as well as the use of technology as a resistance mechanism to traditional oppressive disaster relief practices. And by doing so, they can provide practical solutions to incorporate activism in disaster response, hence expanding the possibility of social justice in the face of natural disasters.

By framing technology as a resistance mechanism, I am suggesting that digital spaces are powerful platforms to showcase local voices and empower local communities during a disaster by sharing information about the aftermath of a calamity with the global community. We need to understand how these actors use different forms of digital media technologies to appreciate people's reactions, sentiments, and networks in a disaster situation. For this work to happen, we need collaborative efforts between academics and practitioners. The disaster relief industry and practitioners can benefit from academic research regarding such local/global crisis communication because large-scale disaster requires a multidimensional rhetorical approach. It is therefore necessary for researchers and practitioners to collectively think about innovative frameworks created by local activists that can help in addressing social injustices during disasters. By introducing a social justice-oriented framework for intervening in disaster rhetoric, we, as researchers and practitioners, would be putting the local narratives of resistance and ways of forming knowledge above implementing what local communities understand as "Western standards of communication and disaster response." By using activist-derived frameworks, we can incorporate social justice-oriented communication and disaster response that will help us in understanding how current disaster relief models strengthen systemic oppressions, creating newer forms of injustice in post-disaster situations. We can also begin to understand alternative humanitarian actions that challenge social injustices in a post-disaster situation. This is why I have worked to establish theoretical, methodological, and practical contributions to scholars, researchers, and practitioners. I have also developed efficient solutions that should help technical communication practitioners, disaster responders, and technology experts respond to a disaster according to a social justice framework that serves as a guide for managing and rethinking the approaches to global disaster management.

## EXPANDING UPON DISASTER RHETORIC AND CRISIS COMMUNICATION

To explore the formation of the coalitions that conducted transnational disaster response, I am extending the theoretical framework of assemblage theory, whose case studies typically draw from Western contexts that would not be applicable when studying transnational contexts. While assemblage theory has been used to understand emergent networks and connections, the theory has often overlooked the transnational contexts, cultures, and languages within the emergent marginalized local disaster activist networks described above. In this way, I concur with Ian Buchanan, one assemblage theory critic, who argued that "if everything is or must be an assemblage then the term loses precision, indeed it loses its analytic power altogether" (391). Assemblage theory has been poised as a tool used to analyze every context, every network, and every incident. It is thus necessary for assemblage theory to become less all-encompassing. It must become more malleable, and flexible, such that the theory itself can expand in its utility. I am proposing that the incorporation of a social justice-oriented framework informed by marginalized experiences is essential if such a theory is to be used to study the rhetoric of disaster.

As such, a grounding in non-Western and decolonial rhetorical as well as theoretical perspectives is necessary to push back against the supremacy of the Western European rhetorical traditions in disaster response and crisis communication to develop a social justice emphasis. Broadly speaking, the Western knowledge-making system grounded in a monolithic worldview delegitimized other ways of knowing as savage, superstitious, and primitive (Akena 600). Such a knowledge-making system was also often considered universal knowledge. When operating in a disaster, applying monolithic and universal knowledge to understanding the local issues and challenges will be harmful. We can argue that due to the phenomenon of globalization, the binary of West and non-West has been blurred (Appadurai), which can be explicitly seen in fashion, trade, and finance. However, in cases of knowledge making and communication by disaster relief agencies, I will demonstrate that there are still Western influences of a similar monolithic worldview where one-size-fits-all kinds of disaster response and communication are more apparent and can be more damaging than supportive. Hence, in this context, I define non-Western disaster response and decolonial disaster response as rhetorical perspectives that help challenge the monolithic/universal knowledge systems and arguments by disaster relief agencies in disaster response.

I will argue that non-Western disaster response is grounded in local community needs and is informed by the sense of collaborative actions that address the injustices that suffering, marginalized communities are forced to endure. This effort, which I term *swa-byabasthapan* (loosely translated as "self-management"), is typically localized and acts as an alternative way to respond to a disaster. *Swa-byabasthapan* entails not waiting for the government, but undertaking actions that lead to organizing and self-managing events during and after disasters. It involves communities working together to achieve the goals they set out for themselves, which, in times of disaster, often involve saving lives and providing aid. Non-Western response strategies are in part influenced by local frameworks, and in part by the opposition to disaster response provided by Western relief organizations or governments. Often the non-Western actors in disaster response might be hidden because of the influences of the presence of Western disaster response mechanisms, people, or ways of thinking. While the Western actors' support in disaster response cannot be denied, this book is only making arguments for recognizing and valuing the work of non-Western actors and working together with them to support humans who are suffering.

*Swa-byabasthapan* will not, however, be used to describe the work of activists in Puerto Rico. The decolonial context in Puerto Rico is different from other parts of the United States. Puerto Rican scholar Teresa Delgado believes that the Puerto Rican people's story of oppression and resistance must be understood in the context of their socio-historical experience of colonization. This is because Puerto Rico is still a US territory and there is a constant struggle for sovereignty from the United States. Karrieann Soto Vega argues that Puerto Ricans and the Puerto Rican diaspora responded to Hurricane Maria via "autogestión" (loosely translated as "self-management") a Puerto Rican concept defined as a coalitional counter-praxis of survival. This counter-praxis allowed for the establishment of newer sovereignty initiatives such as food, territorial, and energy sovereignty (Bonilla; Lloréns; Reyes Curz). Soto Vega further suggests that the disaster response to Hurricane Maria consisted of decolonial performatics and communal acts of place-making. Furthermore, decolonization is a path forward to creating systems that are just and equitable, addressing inequality through education, dialogue, communication, and action ("What Is Decolonization?"). Hence, decolonial disaster response involves communal acts of recognizing the community's needs and supporting such communities by reimagining sovereignty and developing an alternative grassroots disaster response effort that resists the US's colonial power and the Western paradigms of knowledge implemented by the colonizer. Moving forward then, I use both terminologies *swa-byabasthapan* and *autogestión* to further explore the disaster response performed by various actors in both Nepal and Puerto Rico respectively with examples, narratives, and other sources of data.

It is important to acknowledge that in the field of rhetoric as well as technical and professional communication, non-Western and decolonial rhetorical theories and perspectives have come to the forefront due to the work of scholars of the non-Western world and colonized spaces. Comparative rhetoric scholars such as LuMing Mao, Bo Wang, and Keith Lloyd and others have uncovered non-Western ancient texts and traditions, which are then compared to Western texts to challenge the established canons via recontextualization. Moreover, comparative rhetoricians, while researching underrepresented groups, individuals, and spaces, tend to underscore the necessity for researchers to be self-reflexive about their academic training, their cultural background, and how these factors might affect the people and the contexts that they are researching. In addition, Aníbal Quijano argues that decoloniality is needed to clear the way for new intercultural communication, for an interchange of experiences and meanings that provides space and legitimacy for knowledges other than the Eurocentric one (177). Furthermore, Eve Tuck and Wayne Yang emphasize that decolonization takes a different shape in different contexts. For example, in the United States, many Indigenous peoples have been forcibly removed from their homeland. Such forceable removal has led to the destruction of communities. Hence, decolonization in exploitative colonial situations could involve the seizing of imperial wealth by the postcolonial subject (Tuck and Yang 7). In decolonizing knowledge, as Angela Haas suggests, decolonial methodologies could serve to redress colonial influences on the perception of people, literacy, language, culture, and relationships, and support the coexistence of cultures, languages, literacies, memories, and having a reciprocal dialogue between and across them (297). To study transnational contexts and marginalized spaces through assemblage theory, then, we need to be mindful of how current disaster theories forcefully impose Western theories upon non-Western contexts. We too easily dismiss the value of *swa-byabasthapan* and *autogestión* in the name of traditional disaster relief methods.

It is possible, however, to put assemblage theory in the service of activists confronting their marginalization through forming collective responses to disasters. As framed by Gilles Deleuze and Félix Guattari in their book *A Thousand Plateaus*, an assemblage establishes connections among other beings, human and non-human, and it is always in the process of becoming. What Deleuze and Guattari fail to address in their analysis, however, is how this process of becoming spans multiple spaces, countries, cultures, and human and non-human actors across the globe. Furthermore, Manuel DeLanda defines an assemblage as "a multiplicity, which is made up of heterogenous terms and which establishes liaisons, relations between them, across ages, sexes, and reigns—different nature" (1). This definition of an assemblage invites a rethinking of the idea of heterogeneity, one that is informed by the cultural and contextual backgrounds of the people and places where the assemblages form. In the case of disasters, multiple communities perform actions via digital platforms, and that choice helps in establishing the assemblage's identity as being transnational. In the current technological context, these assemblages can either be real (physical) or online. A transnational assemblage is a becoming that brings various human and non-human elements together from multiple geographical, social, and cultural spaces within local communal practices (Slack and Wise). These are moments captured by terms such as *swa-byabasthapan* and *autogestión.*

Acknowledging these non-Western and decolonial perspectives, embedded in such transnational assemblages, will allow us to examine inequality, discrimination, exploitation, and global colonial domination in the Nepalis and Puerto Rican communities with self-reflexivity and without othering the experiences of the people of these spaces (Agboka; Itchuaqiyaq and Matheson; Quijano; B.Wang). Such perspectives allow us to expand to value people and ideas that come from overlooked communities. Thus, I define transnational assemblages in the context of disaster as collectives of people, organizations, or entities who are connected transnationally via online and offline mediums and who gather to respond to a certain situation of natural or political crisis by challenging the dominant narratives and practices. These transnational assemblages are complex because, within these assemblages, transcultural and transdisciplinary interactions occur to address the countless social inequities and injustices brought on by a disaster.

In bringing various elements together, transnational assemblages create a variety of points like a rhizome that help in creating networks to perform "transnational collective action which is coordinated by international campaigns on the part of networks of activists against international actors, other states, or international institutions" (Schell 599). Transnational assemblages therefore bring transnational communities together to coordinate relief, rescue, and community-based campaigns during a disaster by thriving in online spaces such as Facebook or X (formerly Twitter), holding space. Delanda refers to this phenomena as *territorialization,* which refers "not only to the determination of spatial boundaries of a whole—as in the territory of the community, city, or nation-state—but also to the degree to which an assemblage's parts are drawn from a homogenous repertoire or the degree to which an assemblage homogenizes its own component" (DeLanda 22). However, rather than creating a territory, holding space makes for justice-oriented actions and showcases a sense of solidarity. As a transnational assemblage emerges and evolves, some of its links may break at a given spot; within those broken spaces, the rhizome will mend by rebuilding one of its old lines, or it will form new lines by returning to the state that existed before the creation of that part of the assemblage (DeLanda; Deleuze & Guattari). This process is called *deterritorialization*, which may signal the end of networked partnerships or geographical dispersion, or it may signal the elimination of some rituals, which further invites the invention of newer forms of communal participation (DeLanda). However, we can reframe this as moving away to hold other spaces.

As I will discuss in greater detail in later chapters, transnational assemblages are motivated by affect—the cultural, social, and global contexts mediating the way communities interact with one another, and how people outside of these communities support each other. The $17^{th}$-century philosopher Baruch Spinoza defines *affect* as "variations produced in the body by interactions with other bodies, which may lead to increased or diminished activity" (qtd. in Papacharissi, 13). Affect helps human beings act, react, or not act in certain situations. Brian Massumi characterizes affect by recognizing the importance of intensity. Events, incidents, and disasters create spontaneous moments where situations are intense and draw global attention. In transnational assemblages, affect helps bodies react or act to form newer ties or relationships across the globe. Affect helps to form new habits and rituals via intercultural understanding and communications, disrupting the established norms and thus leading toward disaster response that is different from the official one. Affect, as an element of transnational assemblages, could be the perception of a situation that leads to a modification of the body, which then triggers the emotion of consciousness of the mind (Deleuze and Guattari, qtd. in Papacharissi). Thus, the conceptual framing of transnational assemblages helps in understanding how transcultural communities from transnational spaces are motivated by affective reactions created by the event to participate in responding out of a social justice framework to catastrophic disasters.

## CRISIS PUBLICS FOR SOCIAL JUSTICE

Crisis communication and crisis management as a field has been active since the 1980s (Frandsen and Johansen) and has expanded into research, teaching, and a full-time job. However, in the field of rhetoric, writing, and technical communication, though discourse on disaster is evident, there has been less scholarship that directly addresses crisis communication; instead, scholars have written on risk communication

(Grabill and Simmons). W. Timothy Coombs defines crisis communication as "the collection, processing, and dissemination of information required to address a crisis situation" (20). The problem with this definition is that, rather than describing crisis communication that supports people and helps them get accurate information, it mainly characterizes crisis communication as a method for salvaging the image and reputation of a publicly outcast organization or company. A disaster, however, goes beyond an organizational crisis. A disaster also requires communications that help people safeguard their and their loved ones' lives. In contrast to Coombs's definition, Pamela Walaski defines crisis communication as "those messages that are given to audiences during an emergency event that threatens them either immediately or at some foreseeable point in the near future" (9). Effective and accurate communication during a crisis is an essential lifesaving tool as the impacts of catastrophic disasters are ultimately unpredictable and span multiple countries, cultures, and contexts. Therefore, we need a communications mechanism that is more contextual, which is why the traditional definition of crisis communication needs modification.

I argue that crisis communication should be inclusive and social justice-oriented. As such, I argue that transnational assemblages model a form of crisis communication where transnational actors share information, messages, pictures, and data within the varied contexts and multiple languages that incorporate a cultural grounding. This definition goes beyond the traditional interpretation of crisis communication because it acknowledges the entire rhetorical situation that arises amid a calamity. Crisis communication during a disaster is transmitted through both traditional and newer means of communication, such as mobile phones and social media platforms that organizations or transnational assemblages use to communicate in multiple languages. These transnational assemblages are composed of people who represent transcultural communities and have roots in the communities suffering through a disaster. The communications that transnational assemblages perform can take countless multimodal forms, and members of the assemblage can perform such communication both formally and informally. In many cases, transnational assemblages help in identifying the gaps in communication that may be created by the official disaster response system, and they may also encourage actors to stand up for the community. Hence, theorizing transnational assemblages will help us understand the role, work, and contribution of the various transnational actors involved in disaster response efforts. Such a new theoretical framework will lead toward the practical contributions needed to develop effective tools for tackling the challenges of a disaster.

The transnational assemblage theory that I therefore posit is informed by social justice and intersectional frameworks that aid in understanding the dynamic and complex nature of communication during a crisis. These assemblages can be defined as "collectives of people, organizations, or entities, who are connected transnationally via online and offline mediums and who gather to respond to a certain situation of natural or political crisis by challenging the dominant narratives and practices" (Baniya, "Transnational Assemblages" 4). As such, I argue that crisis publics emerge during an emergency not only to facilitate crisis communication in their respective communities, but also to challenge the privileged narratives and to address social injustices created by unequal distribution of aid or information. The crisis publics who emerge on both social media and other offline spaces can help identify the gaps in communication that may arise within the official disaster response systems like governments and humanitarian organizations. Such assemblages highlight and respond to injustices and, as such, such assemblages help communities organize in response to their self-defined needs.

Disasters are uncertain, yet inevitable.
Injustices are apparent, yet solvable.
Assemble *swa-byabasthapan.*
Assemble *autogestión.*

## CHAPTER OVERVIEW

### Chapter 1: Transnational Assemblages in a Globalized World

In Chapter 1, I redefine the traditional concept of the rhetoric of disaster by arguing that, in the contemporary world, such rhetoric is an emerging discourse between, within, and among multiple transnational assemblages across the globe. I extend the concept of transnational assemblages by integrating theories of intersectionality to rethink how coalitional actions are performed globally while marginalized communities respond to their local disaster as well as address social inequities. With this grounding, I show that disaster rhetoric is shaped by flows and networks of communications as well as affective engagements in both online and offline spaces. I end by introducing the mixed-methods research approach of narrative inquiry and social network analysis to frame how the Nepal and Puerto Rico case studies were developed. The following chapters then apply transnational assemblage theory to the specific natural disasters faced by these communities.

### Chapter 2: Non-Western Disaster Response during the April 25, 2015 Nepal Earthquake

In Chapter 2, I conduct a detailed case study of the Nepal earthquake and provide an overview of how Nepalis and global actors responded to this disaster. This chapter describes how Nepalis and various international actors responded to the disaster by using various internet-based technologies and social media platforms like Facebook, Twitter, Instagram, WhatsApp, and blogs. I present an analysis of the interviews I conducted with 14 individuals (both Nepalis and non-Nepalis) who showcased rhetorical agency in supporting their communities either by forming transnational assemblages or by being a part of such transnational assemblages. I also present the results of a social network analysis of millions of tweets that were posted during the first week of the Nepal earthquake to show how digital platforms like Twitter help in motivating and regulating the transnational assemblages when responding to a crisis. With these results, this chapter introduces the non-Western ways of disaster response and argues that, while a larger formal global disaster response happens, various local contexts and knowledge are ignored, thus leading toward the marginalization of vulnerable communities.

### Chapter 3: Decolonial Approaches to Disaster Response during Hurricane Maria in Puerto Rico

Chapter 3 focuses on Hurricane Maria in Puerto Rico and provides an overview of decolonial approaches to disaster response. I also discuss the background and a historical overview of colonialism and how such a political situation exacerbated the consequences of Hurricane Maria. As in the previous chapter, this case study will highlight how Puerto Ricans resisted colonial practices by not relying on the government and by forming transnational assemblages. I present the results of my narrative inquiry, which involved 14 Puerto Rican activists, community-based organizers, and journalists, to showcase the survival practices of marginalized communities who have navigated the oppressive systems to restore peace and stability in their society. I also focus on presenting an analysis of millions of tweets that were posted during the first week of Hurricane Maria to show how people in Puerto Rico and around the globe participated in responding to the disaster. With these results, this chapter introduces the decolonial approaches of disaster response and how Puerto Ricans used digital technologies to respond to the crisis their communities were facing.

**Chapter 4: Social Justice-Oriented Technical Communications in Global Disaster Management**

In Chapter 4, I offer both theoretical and practical contributions to make a case for why social justice-oriented technical communication is necessary for global disaster management, and I present how researchers and practitioners can take up this call in managing a future disaster. With this demonstration, I argue that there is an urgency for the field to explore how global technical communications praxis helps to address injustices in a contemporary networked world. I further this argument to showcase how technical communicators can perform transdisciplinary research in disaster management to minimize the impacts of catastrophic disasters affecting the world's most vulnerable populations. I conclude that intersectionality and a social justice framework will help in contextualizing information based on the local context, finding various places where marginalization may occur. I also describe ways to identify and work with various transnational assemblages, create strategies to work with the community organizers, and lead disaster response efforts by putting the local knowledge at the center of all endeavors. This chapter ends with takeaways where I will suggest some strategies for developing social justice-oriented technical communication for practitioners. I also lay the groundwork for future studies and incorporate pedagogical implications of this research in various university courses.

# 1

## Transnational Assemblages in a Globalized World

When I started my PhD studies in 2016, memories of the Nepal earthquake were still very fresh in my mind, and I could not ignore them. My academic investment in rhetorical theories and technical and professional communication (TPC) made me contemplate and critically think about my response to the catastrophe. I was a journalist, communications practitioner, and active social media user during the time of the earthquake. Through these professional and personal practices, I have been an active responder to the disaster and its consequences in Nepal where I was part of broadcasting news via Radio Nepal and participated in disaster relief via an organization named Teach for Nepal. As I started to rhetorically think about my personal experiences, rhetorical studies of disaster became my area of focus through which I was able to remain connected with my community and country. While I was studying the Nepal earthquake, other disasters were happening around the world. I knew that smaller countries and marginalized spaces tended to suffer the most when disasters occurred because such communities lack the infrastructure and finances necessary to respond to a catastrophic calamity. When Hurricane Maria struck in late September 2017, for example, news and information about Puerto Rico started to fill my social media feed. As a rhetorician, I started to recognize similarities and differences between the Nepal earthquake and Hurricane Maria.

Disaster research is challenging not only because it is associated with the destruction of lives and infrastructures, but also because it involves researching an entire ecosystem and its actors. Today's disaster experiences are recorded in digital mediums in the form of narratives. Such experiences, both official and unofficial, help in shaping knowledge during a disaster. Liza Potts suggests that during a disaster, "unlike prior experiences in which users marched through a set of interfaces and stayed contained within systems, social web participants consider an entire ecosystem of solutions for communicating with others across multiple networks" (*Social Media in Disaster Response* 18). In such ecosystems, rhetoric "never escapes from world into social or the symbolic: it is always worldly, a dynamic, emergent composite of meaning and matter" (Rickert 222). As one of the actors in the disaster ecosystem myself, I accepted the challenge to understand the rhetoric of disaster by seeking, finding, and listening to the narratives of other actors. The phrase *rhetoric of disaster* has previously appeared in an article by Michael F. Bernard-Donals in 2001 where he focuses on Holocaust testimonials and traces the origin of rhetoric of disaster in Maurice Blanchot by arguing that the consequences of a rhetoric of disaster are troubling. Bernard-Donals's theorization of the concept of rhetoric of disaster differs from my conceptualization as his mostly focused on archives whereas I extend this concept by focusing on theorizing rhetoric of disaster as a discourse mediated via various digital and nondigital systems. More specifically, I wanted to highlight people and the actions they demonstrated in the aftermath of the Nepal earthquake and Hurricane Maria and how they contributed in forming a rhetoric of disaster.

As a researcher educated mostly from a Western point of view, I had never been trained to think about the non-Western world from a non-Western point of view or understand values of such a point of view. I found it challenging to conceptualize the appropriate methods to undertake such work. Scholar Bo Wang has talked about similar transcultural challenges in her research, highlighting the need for deeply reflective and reflexive practices when developing new interpretive frameworks for research across cultural, geographical, and disciplinary boundaries. Likewise, Mary Garrett states that "speaking for/about an underrepresented tradition or group especially calls for self-reflexivity because of the insulating effects of good intentions" (251). Yet, when I began to explore the sites of this study, I often found myself thinking within familiar theoretical lenses learned in graduate school. As an emerging researcher in a non-Western rhetorical field, I had to challenge my own Western education, forcing myself to move away from preconceived notions and toward a research method that would highlight the community and its very unique and individual perspectives.

I found it difficult to think outside of the theories and frameworks produced by the "canon" of Western theorists. Expanding my framework as a researcher, I challenged myself with the following methodological and ethical questions:

- How can I conduct research on my own community while I compare them to a community that I am not a part of by deepening reflexivity and becoming more mindful of my own biases because of my subjectivities?
- How do I negotiate the education I have received from the West and put it in conversation with my non-Western education while creating a balance between them?
- How can I move toward bridging the gap between Western and non-Western theoretical and methodological practices?

These questions have allowed me to analyze the communities' perspectives in a different light, enabling the prioritization of community voices. As Patricia Sullivan and James Porter argue, "research practices should be understood as complex actions that are taken in situation, that arise out of who we are and what we believe" (4). Indeed, throughout the research process, I have adopted reflexivity within my own research practices in searching for participants, reaching out to them, interviewing them, and analyzing the data. And I have been constantly guided by my own sense of responsibility to the world's most marginalized communities. As such, this project is grounded in avoiding dominant cultural frameworks, practices, and contexts in the understanding of disaster response. It challenges the contemporary work in disaster response that is mediated through Western philosophy, financial support, and organization. Hence, in this research, I highlight the voices of people who emerged as the transnational assemblages who, during times of two disasters, supported their communities' survival. The phrase *transnational assemblages* has appeared in research by Vrushali Patil and Bandana Purkayastha where they present a case study of a rape in India in the year 2012 and how it created affective cultural and transnational assemblages. In this book, I make this choice to create space for the transnational assemblages in the context of disaster and actors within these assemblages who play a vital role in managing the disaster response work.

To highlight underrepresented perspectives, I conceptualized the rhetoric of disaster in a globalized context by arguing that such rhetoric of disaster is an emerging discourse between, within, and among multiple transnational assemblages around the globe. I also introduce the concept of transnational assemblages by grounding in the theories of intersectionality to rethink how coalitional actions performed globally by marginalized communities responding to their local disaster affect the global narrative. With this grounding, I argue that established formal organizations that lead disaster response efforts where disaster rhetoric circulates often ignore the agency and needs of marginalized communities, overlooking such communities' tactical and strategic interventions via networks of communications and affective engagements in both online and offline spaces. In the globalized world, disaster multiplies the effect of transnational coalitional actions by causing sudden shifts in the rhetorical situation, by breaking boundaries, and by allowing for the emergence of various transnational assemblages. In effect, I use the concept of transnational assemblage to help understand the systems of oppressions that exacerbate the effects of a disaster and to accentuate the power of the local community's response efforts. Additionally, I have used a mixed-methods study of narrative inquiry and social network analysis to complement my theoretical approach, which I discuss toward the end of this chapter. My research question was designed to look for the formation and mobilization of transnational assemblages after the disaster. The research question and the rigorousness of the research demanded two epistemological routes for my study: qualitative and quantitative. Combining these two research methods helped me gain different perspectives about how transnational networks function on a people-to-people level and how they function on a societal, cultural, and global level. And in the conclusion of the chapter, I discuss the reflexive research method that allowed these insights to be developed.

## THE RHETORIC OF DISASTER IN A NETWORKED, TECHNOLOGICAL, GLOBALIZED WORLD

The rhetoric of disaster in the digitally complex, networked, and technological world is embedded in three overarching geopolitical and technological phenomena:

1. globalization that creates intersections of identities, nationalities, and genders among the transcultural diasporic communities, thus disrupting physical and cultural boundaries;
2. rhetorical actions and ecologies that are mediated by the spontaneous formation of transnational assemblages via affect and disseminated by digital technologies; and

3. bureaucratic networks of governmental and non-governmental humanitarian mechanisms which are on high-alert and they do function; yet, they become dysfunctional due to the scale and consequences of disaster that they can never handle entirely.

Unexpected disasters create a knowledge vacuum that instigates spontaneous actions across these domains through affective connections mediated across platforms, space, and time zones, resulting in transnational coalitions (Baniya "Transnational Assemblages"). Assemblage theory can help in exploring the complexities of the formation and expansion of these networks and flows of communication during a disaster response situation. When a disaster strikes, however, there are multiple stakeholders who represent varied disciplinary, cultural, and educational backgrounds that come into play. To fully understand a complex global disaster requires a theoretical framework that incorporates the varied intersections of disciplines, expertise, and non-Western and decolonial perspectives.

The creation of transnational assemblages and the rhetoric of disaster produced by them in a digital world is mitigated by "the speed and spread of the Internet and the simultaneous comparative growth in travel, cross-cultural media, and global advertisement" (Appadurai 61). The rise of the internet has created a digitally connected world that reacts to disaster in transcultural ways within a very limited amount of time. Zizi Papacharissi adds, "The Internet reorganizes the flows of time and space in ways that promise greater autonomy but also conform to the habitus of practices, hierarchies, and structures that form its historical context" (7). During a time of disaster and emergency, digital media creates an ambient environment (Rickert) by bringing people together via technologies and by creating different practices and structures that start circulating throughout the world.

Current information and communication technologies are a means for saving lives and helping people in the wake of a disaster. Peter K. Haff argues that the proliferation of technology across the globe defines the Technosphere—the assemblage of large-scale, networked technologies that can make things possible through nearly instantaneous communication and mass distribution. In the context of a disaster, people's lives depend on instantaneous communication mechanisms to communicate and connect with other people around the globe. Such assemblages bring both human and non-human elements together via instant communication technologies so that actors may share information, network, volunteer, and raise funds. Transnational assemblages create rhetorics of disaster. For example, the tweets, replies to tweets, and retweets with hashtags like #NepalEarthquake and #HurricaneMaria created communication channels among countless human users by fostering sentimental connections that are made possible thanks to physical, non-human networks such as mobile towers, machines, and satellites. As Jane Bennett confirms, assemblages include humans and their constructions, but they also include some very active and powerful non-humans: electrons, trees, wind, and electromagnetic fields. Such networked assemblages are material in nature and provide "agential possibilities and responsibilities for reconfiguring the material-social relations of the world" (Barad, *Meeting the Universe Halfway* 241).Transnational assemblages shrink physical distance by connecting people via social media, shift the relationship between producers and consumers, and blur the lines between temporary locales and the national attachments (Appadurai). Those national attachments, concerns, and empathetic connections in return help in the creation of assemblages consisting of volunteers, donors, information curators, and medical professionals that respond to a disaster and help "their fellow" communities that are suffering.

The rhetoric of disaster in a networked, technological, and globalized world is therefore motivated by affect and disseminated by social media. For instance, a picture of a Nepali woman who was found under piles of rubble was posted on Twitter via a phone or laptop. This picture created an emotional response in someone living in the United States, who, upon seeing the image, decided to find a GoFundMe page dedicated to collecting contributions for relief efforts in response to the Nepal earthquake. This person sent the money they earned to support relief, thus participating in a giving culture or philanthropic activity, which was initiated due to the disaster. This calamity subsequently became a part of the collective memory imprinted in our psyches and recycled on media platforms, rendering the disaster a permanent part of our history and identity (Papacharissi, "Affective Publics" 2). In this way, the person donating the money has become a part of a transnational assemblage that is responding to a disaster on the ground. It is with the support of that person's money, which flows through various channels, that aid has the possibility to reach a person suffering through the consequences of a terrible disaster. For that aid to reach and support the person, there are various rhetorical decisions that must be made: what photo to post, how to caption the photo, what platform to use. With effective rhetorical decisions, many assemblages that result from affect have the agency to perform tasks that are not being handled by formal institutions, such as the government.

As such, the rhetoric of disaster disrupts physical foundations and geographical boundaries within differing social, political, and economic spaces. This disruption creates various "flows" that help in reinventing the discourse of the disaster, which is fluid and always emerging (DeLanda). It also creates newer ways for people who are very far away from the location affected by the calamity to act, address others, and mitigate the challenges of the disaster. José Miguel Albala-Bertrand argues that "[g]lobalization is a societal process that widens and deepens the interactions between each country and the rest of the world" (147). The rhetoric of disaster motivates people around the globe to be a part of a transnational assemblage by creating flows that engage people in the discourse and by connecting actors with the vulnerable locals. As Albala-Bertrand explains, "In general, these interconnections refer to the institutions associated with the flows of goods, services, people, information, and cultural traits in a worldwide context" (147). In other words, flows are not just associated with official institutions. They are associated with people and the assemblages created by them and for them to share information, to act together. For instance, in both the Nepal and Puerto Rico disasters, not just established organizations but transnational assemblages ensured relief materials such as food, water, tarpaulins, and medical supplies were arriving from all over the world. Countless people from around the globe either engaged with the disaster response efforts online or physically by going to the disaster sites to help people in need. Through effective rhetorical practices, these flows are expedited by the circulation of information and communications that happens in digital spaces, creating affective connections among people through narratives, thus allowing the "global" to participate in the "local" affected by the disaster.

In effect, a disaster initiates the creation of a global culture that helps transnational assemblages thrive and territorialize. This ecosystem is mostly mediated via computerized technologies that expedite the process of sharing, interacting, and participating in the culture. An example of such a culture could be as simple as changing one's profile picture on Facebook to one that includes a "Pray for Nepal" frame or the culture of creating hashtags like #NepalEarthquake, #PuertoRicoRiseUp,

#NepalRises, and #HurricaneMaria. The response of this culture is instantaneous, and narratives and stories with the human element are transformed into data, voices, videos, pictures, and emotions. Data is therefore humanized, and subjectivity is computerized, thus allowing humans to join in and be a part of the transnational assemblage (Hayles 39). Bruno Latour argues that "we don't assemble because we agree, look alike, feel good, are socially compatible, or wish to fuse together, but because we are brought by divisive matters of concern into some neutral, isolated place in order to come to some sort of provisional makeshift (dis)agreement" (3). When disaster happens, boundaries are blurred and it becomes a global phenomenon where people, despite differences in culture, geographical locations, economic statues, and expertise, are assembled and are motivated to work together in solving the disruptions created by the disaster.

The agential possibilities of transnational assemblages create different contact zones and create boundaries where the global and local populations come together to form a collective globalized action composed of actors responding to the tragedy. Karen Barad in her article "Posthuman Performativity . . ." argues that "it is through specific agential intra-actions that the boundaries and properties of the 'components' of phenomena become determinate and that particular embodied concepts become meaningful" (815). For example, even though the disasters happened in physical locations, users from around the world instantly reached to local community members and supported them by using various digital technologies and the components which help in embodying the concept of disaster response. That support and its users represented both official and unofficial sectors that demonstrated agency and took responsibility for faster rescue and relief operations. By accelerating their work, communication technologies helped actors connect with people working on the ground as well as with people experiencing and suffering through the aftermath of the disasters. Indeed, Bennett believes that the distinctive efficacy of a working whole made up of somatic, technological, cultural, and atmospheric elements is the agency of assemblages. These elements allow people to connect, interact, and engage in creating ambient contact zones that include aspects like feeling, mood, intuition, and decision-making. Thomas J. Rickert says, "[A]mbience involves more than just the whole person, as it were; the ambience is inseparable from the person in the environment that gives rise to ambience" (8). In other words, ambience during a disaster develops among people who are suffering and the people who want to support those who are suffering. This relationship leads actors to make decisions based on connections established via, and expedited by, social media. Such decisions, which are faster in times of struggle, were part of the process when actors responding to the Nepal earthquake and Hurricane Maria worked to undertake activities like organizing relief, volunteering, fundraising, and curating information.

Rhetorics of disaster initiate rhetorical interactions and actions from various sociopolitical contexts and often from people with intersectional identities across time and space. While the rhetorical theories might help in exploring the complexities of the formation and expansion of the networks and flows of communications that occur in response to a calamity, understanding the rhetoric of disaster is a complex task. It requires an understanding of the varied intersections of perspectives that are affected by culture, language, and rhetorical contexts, identities, race, class, genders including the nature and type of any disaster itself. This is because the systems of oppression get materialized in the newer context of disaster and affect the most marginalized and vulnerable populations. With climate change and the frequency of disasters in the world that create severe impacts in vulnerable communities, we need to establish mechanisms to understand not only how to respond to the consequences of compounding disasters, but also to understand how we can challenge the systems of oppression that exacerbate the impacts of such crises, especially to the marginalized and vulnerable populations. While the rhetoric of disaster functions differently in situations of disaster, the understanding of how it functions in any kind of disaster will help prepare in non-disaster situations. As the rhetoric of disaster keeps on evolving, we need a transnational assemblage framework that can help us understand disaster rhetorics in a more nuanced way, grounding the disaster response efforts and related rhetorics in the community and in the people responding to a disaster. Doing so will help us identify systems of oppression by understanding resistances, actions, and interactions amongst people.

## Transnational Assemblages in Disaster Rhetorics

Disasters create ecological disturbances by shifting geographies, displacing lives, and destroying infrastructures. During these chaotic times, an ecology comes into existence in the form of assemblages

(DeLanda) of both human and non-human actors (Latour) often mediated by social, communal, and technological networks. As technology has advanced, scholars in rhetoric as well as technical and professional communication have studied networks, ecologies, and the transformation of these networked spaces. This "ecological turn" in rhetoric and writing has led scholars to analyze public distribution models of writing during disasters as they relate to issues of agency, public sphere, networks, and ambience (Edbauer; Cooper; Rickert; Edwards and Lang). Ongoing world events, such as protest movements and uprisings, have motivated scholars to study the relevance of networked connections, communications, and agency. Madison Jones states, "Today, ecology is a threshold concept, offering a rhetorical framework which indexes the study of networked discourse, new materialism, and systems thinking . . . and connotes many types of relational systems" (5). Similarly, Dan Ehrenfeld argues that the ecological turn is not a radical break from foundational models of public sphere but a deeper engagement toward how strangers enact their relations with one another via ecology, network, or systems (307). Such concepts spontaneously come into existence in the aftermath of a disaster as they circulate globally within and beyond digital infrastructures initiating communities, coalitions, or assemblages. Hence, moving toward rhetorical ecologies helps us understand how events (like disasters) extend beyond the limits of spatial-temporal boundaries (Edbauer 20). In vulnerable situations, then, "networked publics," composed of journalists, social media users, government officials, healthcare providers, volunteers, and the affected population, conduct "networked actions," such as volunteering, requesting aid, and donating, thus becoming transnational assemblages. These assemblages are material in nature, and, in a digitally advanced world, they are robust because of technologies such as the internet, mobile phones, and the digital social web (Bennett).

As discussed previously, the dominant version of assemblage theory explains that networks are formed via personal, social, and technological interactions. According to Deleuze and Guattari, an assemblage establishes connections among multiplicities, and it is always in the process of becoming or emerging. An assemblage is always in the process of becoming when it establishes its existence by interacting with other beings—both human and non-human. An assemblage is rhizomatic in its ability to emerge and spread. In assemblage theory, a rhizome is a networking mechanism that helps connect one entity (human or non-human) to the others in the assemblage. Deleuze and Guattari suggest that a rhizome has no beginning nor end because "it is always in the middle, between things, interbeing, intermezzo" (25). An assemblage is therefore adaptable, connectable, and accessible to many people, organizations, and entities that are responding to a greater phenomenon like a disaster. The emergence of an assemblage happens within boundaries that are created in physical space, such as a community, city, or nation-state; it can happen within boundaries in online spaces, such as a Facebook group, a group message chain, and a specific hashtag on Twitter; or an assemblage can even emerge within a combination of both physical and virtual spaces. In any case, Deleuze and Guattari suggest that the process of emergence can be described as "territorialization," by which an assemblage establishes its identity by claiming space.

Manuel DeLanda further elaborates upon the concept of territorialization by explaining that territorialization refers "not only to the determination of spatial boundaries of a whole—as in the territory of the community, city, or nation-state—but also to the degree to which an assemblage's component parts are drawn from a homogenous repertoire, or the degree to which an assemblage homogenizes its own component" (22). In other words, an assemblage creates or claims certain spaces by self-organizing, which involves establishing rules, regulations, and traditions. As an assemblage continues to emerge and evolve though, some of its links to other rhizomes may break; within those broken spaces, the rhizome will mend by either rebuilding one of its old connections, or it will form new connections by returning to the state that existed prior to the creation of that part of the assemblage (DeLanda; Deleuze and Guattari). This process is called "deterritorialization." Deterritorialization makes the assemblage lose its influence, such that the components of the assemblage seek other flows, or points of connection. This means that components can either join a different assemblage or they can create a new one by reinventing their relationship to other elements in the assemblage. While the current assemblage theory allows us to understand the multiplicity of society and concepts such as rhizome, territorializing, and deterritorialization, it somehow fails to deeply explore and understand how the rhetoric of each disaster is different and how in the transnational context such rhizomatic assemblages evolve, become, or emerge. Furthermore, using assemblage theory during a disaster, specifically in a transnational context, needs an expansion into transnational assemblages so that we understand rhetoric of disaster in transnational contexts.

Thus, it is also important to consider that, since disasters and their consequences are location- and context-specific, responding to them requires first responders, which include government employees, nongovernmental agencies, informal networks of volunteers and activists, and community members, to become enculturated. Fortunately, in current disaster situations, because unofficial networks and transnational assemblages are formed via interpersonal, social, and technological spheres, that seems to better acknowledge the networked rhetorical situation, cultural and language differences, thus better adjusting to the needs of the affected community. These assemblages would represent new "territorializations." The existing "territories, assemblages, are the established and structured organizations that take the form of a cluster" (DeLanda 20). Such clusters might act in a more formal way that is forced to follow certain required protocols but that may not actually provide the support the suffering community needs at the time it needs it. Given this consideration, our understanding of an assemblage must go beyond the current research examples, such as disaster organizations. We must consider the rhetorical situation of the affected community and their ability to be agents, to respond to a disaster by holding space and by using varied available technologies. To achieve this new definition, there should be a transnational integration into the power networks of community leaders, volunteers, and responders that support marginalized communities. Therefore, there should be a redefinition of assemblage, one that recognizes how transnational communities can act unhindered by established protocols for their own survival.

The current specific framing of assemblages does not allow scholars to gain a deeper understanding of the culture, context, and, most important, the systems of oppression that some networked mechanisms can perform. Existing rhetorical and communication scholarship has focused on the study of networks, ecology, and assemblages to understand social movements, hashtag/digital activism, activist rhetorics, and coalition formations. It has focused on how a collective affective economy creates participatory actions and interactions. Oftentimes, however, varied forms of oppression are performed through similar historical networks, which are unfortunately overlooked by rhetoric scholars. And non-Western, decolonial, and transnational scholars have also pointed out that while conducting rhetorical research concerning grassroots communities, activism requires careful study of the histories, contexts, and struggles of the affected community. Nikki Sanchez in her TED Talk video reminds us that "decolonization is a work that belongs to all of us." Hence, we need to learn how to study and create a "good assemblage," as Kristin L. Arola and Adam C. Arola argue. Here, a good assemblage is responsive in addressing the social justice needs of a people by enacting new functions and articulations. Such work should contain an acknowledgment of histories of place, activism, and struggle (Soto Vega) as well as an understanding of how techno-material infrastructures characterize national sentiment, people's sense of belonging, and the diaspora (Z.Wang). Then, informed by intersectionality and non-Western or decolonial rhetorics, a newer conceptual "assemblage" research framework would consider how transnational perspectives will help in understanding the discursive patterns that are formed across online and physical spaces by marginalized communities to address the consequences of catastrophic disasters.

## Transnational Connectivities: Building Coalitions across Borders

Transnational assemblages, then, formed in response to a disaster, act as an active site of critical engagement with global power, asymmetries, and inequalities which Bo Wang reminds us should be considered as "coeval contributions to knowledge about transnational rhetoric" (136). Events, incidents, and happenings force the emergence or evolution of a transnational assemblage as it creates spontaneous moments where situations are intense and require the attention of people who can address such circumstances with the help of technology. Such assemblages help in building coalitions through transnational connections among people across borders, languages, cultures, and contexts. Such connections are shaped by the transnational affect that "may involve bodies passing from one state to another as a result of transnational interactions on a computer or mobile phone screen" as well as differing social media platforms, websites, and applications (Leurs 95). Jenny Rice suggests that "affect is not a personal feeling but is instead the means through which bodies act in context with each other" (203). Affect in a transnational assemblage helps in creating flows within and among people and motivates them to take an action and develop a rhetorical communication and disaster response mechanism that is flexible in nature. Such rhetoric, therefore, creates a space that invites and encourages digital or nondigital actions.

The idea of transnational connections that help create a space for actions replaces the language of "territorializing," which implies "taking over," and generates a space for coalitional building, which is necessary when addressing complex situations like a disaster. Such transnational rhetoric *enables* interventions that build coalitions across borders by using differing digital tools to establish networked connections, which aid in a) sharing information about health, food, security, and people's needs; b) confronting unjust practices or inequalities that are often ignored; and c) supporting communities by collecting resources (monetary and non-monetary) from a variety of sources across the world. This intersectional approach, that primarily focuses on coalition-forming as opposed to solely focusing on territorializing, helps in acknowledging that those who are marginalized and who live with various experiences of oppression. This approach also recognizes that effective activism and social transformation can be achieved through coalitional thinking that helps in the formation of a collective force against oppression (Walton et al.).

Importantly, this framework also values the oppressed knowledges of marginalized communities. The transnational affective connectivities that emerge in the aftermath of a calamity and that help build coalitions across borders result in enclaves. Karma Chávez reminds us that "[w]ith coalition-building, in particular, enclaves function as a site of meaning production" (13). Such coalitions help to disrupt the traditional beliefs, power flows, and established protocols. Papacharissi calls such disruptions "'[a]ffective gestures' [that] contribute to spheres of political expression in ways that pluralize, organize, and disrupt conversations" (28). Gestures that form enclaves could be recognized as what Chávez suggests to be the center of social movement and counter-public scholarship. Technology becomes both space and medium, where affective response helps in creating conversations among people of multiple cultures as they interact with each other through their transnational connectivities to form "nontraditional" communal frameworks. Additionally, such conversations and interactions lead to disaster response efforts that involve actions like volunteering, fundraising, curating informational materials, and supporting communities in need that traditional disaster relief organizations fail to undertake. Indeed, during a crisis, spontaneous coalitions that are formed via transnational affect and connectivities require forms of labor, such as digital labor, care, and empathetic labor, that attempt to highlight unjust practices that happen as an aftereffect of catastrophes (Leurs).

In detaching themselves from the traditional disaster framework and assembling into another, the rhetorical agency of each assemblage plays a vital role in shaping the narratives that impact disaster rhetoric. Amy Koerber defines rhetorical agency as "negotiation among competing alternative discourses, that grants individuals some ability to reject discursive elements that they find problematic" (94). Transnational assemblages do not abide by one narrative because that one narrative is typically the inaccurate, official narrative. Instead, transnational assemblages utilize their rhetorical agency, powered by the privileges of access and knowledge of how to use technology and their time dedicated to labor in digital spaces, to search for multiple narratives and tell the marginalized community members' real stories. Transnational assemblages transfer their actions so that actors may closely listen to their communities, interact with the community members and leaders, and create a place for unidentified, unofficial, and difficult counterstories (Martinez) that deserve their own space. Additionally, actors' self-organized assemblages exhibit rhetorical agency by displaying what Natasha N. Jones in her article "Rhetorical Narratives of Black Entrepreneurs" refers to as "a) an awareness of the rhetorical situation, including exigency, Kairos, and an understanding of existing discourses or arguments, and b) the ability, opportunity, or rhetorical space to act" (325). Transnational assemblages during a disaster dig across the system to gain an understanding of the rhetorical situation and share such understanding with the public to motivate people and the institutional system to act and interact with the affected community.

Technological apparatuses further enhance assemblages' rhetorical activities thanks to their ability to share alternative narratives from the affected communities and the work completed by these assemblages. Cheryl Geisler suggests that the concept of rhetorical agency *also* concerns itself with another set of nontraditional contexts—those connected with media. This connection of, for example, sharing photographs, information, or videos via the internet "call[s] attention to the complex ways that rhetorical agency may be dispersed, as a series of articulated networks that connect speakers and hearers in multiple ways" (Geisler 11). The transnational assemblages' disaster response is nontraditional, articulated in various forms of rhetorical agency, and enacted to navigate the complex systems and rhetorical situations. Carolyn Miller has argued that such agency is a property of the rhetorical event, and, disaster becomes the event that motivates people to move beyond their regular life and toward showcasing their rhetorical capacity to perform across geographical boundaries, time zones, and cultural and language barriers. Marilyn Cooper argues that "complex systems (an organism, a matter of concern) are self-organizing: order (and change) results from an ongoing process in which multitude of agents interact frequently and which the results of interactions feed back into process" (421). Some examples of rhetorical agencies displayed by the actors involved in disaster response efforts included not waiting for the government before beginning to help each other, joining or forming groups to self-organize rescue and relief work, motivating themselves to save lives and support people in need, and creating opportunities for outsiders to make donations by using assorted technologies. As Cooper further notes, actors, or agents, are entities that act; by virtue of their action, actors necessarily bring about changes, and such actions during a disaster can come in the form of highlighting inequalities, decentralizing aid, raising funds, and curating information. This becomes important in disaster response as various issues of social justice arise during a disaster, and transnational assemblages could establish themselves as a force to challenge the systems that disregard community needs and well-being.

### Intersections of Communities and Identities

Transnational assemblages are characterized by intersections of communities, cultural identities, and global cultural flows, which is why the theory of transnational assemblages should be grounded in the theory of intersectionality. The grounding in intersectionality helps us perceive that social problems and injustices, along with race, gender, caste, and sexuality, are interconnected with each other (Crenshaw, Collins). The intersectional approach to disaster response helps in understanding advocacy and activism that create room for coalitions across different positionalities, geographies, cultures, and contexts (Yam). Transnational assemblages are formed via the interconnections of culture, identities, and groups of people who are invested in supporting communities in need. Despite differences, transnational assemblages come together by recognizing the interconnectedness of people, social problems, and ideas, which intersectionality helps recognize as a form of critical inquiry and praxis (Collins). Given that this critical inquiry and praxis typically forms spontaneously in a complex environment and situation, transnational assemblages help when examining the interlocking networks of power that influence disaster response efforts, the circulation of disaster discourse, and the relationship among disaster responders, humanitarian actors, governmental networks, and volunteers (Yam). Disaster response can never be achieved with one sole actor, organization, or community; it requires the involvement of multiple organizations, people, and actors across the globe. Hence, disaster response is chaotic and complex. Approaching this work from an intersectional point of view helps in identifying alternative perspectives that recognize how a disaster instigates social problems with deeper roots that should be handled with nuanced critical inquiry and problem-solving approaches. In the context of Nepal, for example, I found that social problems involving caste and geographical location were exacerbated by the earthquake. The same can be said for Black communities, women, the elderly, and people living in remote locations throughout Puerto Rico in the aftermath of Hurricane Maria.

Transnational assemblages bring people from different cultural contexts, language abilities, perspectives, places, and times together in a space where intersectionality enables them to share points of view that are formerly forbidden, outlawed, or simply obscured, creating a platform where uncomfortable conversations can occur. Therefore, transnational assemblages become that space where difficult conversations have a chance to take place, and they create an opportunity for such conversations to be addressed and acknowledged. As we think about transcultural spaces from a non-Western perspective, we can see how global forces create these spaces by circulating information, messages, and collective challenges (Appadurai). In these spaces, what Arjun Appadurai calls "production of localities," human beings exercise their social, technical, and imaginative capacities, including the capacity for violence, warfare, and ecological selfishness (66). In extending such capacities, various transcultural forces unite to work against the systematic violence or warfare present in a community affected by a disaster. Such connections are established via affective emotions that become a global force, disrupting the systems of oppression, injustices, and marginalization.

While transnational assemblages can form transnational connectivities, they can also disconnect. To disconnect, these assemblages either quickly disperse and expand their space for multiplicity or they simply remove themselves, seizing to exist. This phenomenon replaces the idea of deterritorializing. Potts argues that the communities that form in the wake of a disaster quickly disperse. This idea of disconnections helps in identifying patterns from which connections are established, how such connections lose their significance, how they become disconnected, and how they once again reconnect. In a disaster, connections are established based on the immediate needs of the afflicted community. As that immediate need is satisfied, that connection loses its significance until it completely disconnects once the need is entirely satisfied. However, beyond the immediate needs of the community, there are also other larger needs that must be addressed. While this book only concerns itself with the urgency in which transnational assemblages are formed, what happens after the disconnection and urgent needs are met and the community is going through recovery and reconstruction is something that scholars can explore.

## METHODOLOGICAL APPROACH: MIXED-METHODS APPROACH

Achieving the research goals contained in the concept of "transnational assemblages" ultimately comes down to a question of research methodology. Any methodology chosen would require consideration of what socially just and culturally appropriate approach could be used to explore such transnational events, people, and work. Traditionally, when researching underrepresented groups, individuals, and spaces, researchers tend to be self-reflexive about their academic training, their cultural background, and how this background might affect the people and the contexts they are researching. As a researcher invested in community work, I also chose to adopt a self-reflexive methodology that would produce unbiased research concerning two different marginalized communities while simultaneously negotiating my own training in the Western institution with my upbringing and years of professional field work as a journalist and communications practitioner in the non-Western context in Nepal. Furthermore, my lived experiences as a disaster responder in the role as a journalist, and communications practitioner and as a PhD holder are also entangled in this research. Yet, Chanon Adsanatham argues that "the reflexive act [allows] for troubling our own mode of thinking through comparative analysis that critically attends to historicity, specificity, and incongruity in our own tradition and others" (77). Hence, in methodologically conducting this research, I have been aware of my standpoint on highlighting marginalized experiences in disaster response and my subjectivities that come from my cultural, professional, and educational background as a researcher and also a disaster responder.

Through reflexivity, then, I trouble my own thinking and constantly push myself when making methodological decisions in collecting, analyzing, and writing about the data concerning these two communities. I constantly approach the work in a way that highlights the participants and their stories, rather than me and my subjectivities. I took a long way around this approach where I learned from my past work and approaches as a practitioner. I have told this story elsewhere (Baniya et al.). For this book project, I wanted to do radically different things to prioritize people's voices and stories, and since I have more autonomy in my own research project, this was possible. From the very beginning of this project, however, I wanted to work and conduct this research with self-reflexivity. Hence, it was important in this research to avoid the surface-level analysis. Here, in each participant's story that I have collected, I have provided them space to tell their stories. And I wanted the theory to develop from the stories rather than an application of any theoretical framework.

Beyond self-reflection, my methodological intervention included both qualitative and quantitative research methods. Combined, these methods allowed me to gain a nuanced understanding of how to listen to and represent marginalized voices while also analyzing a large data set that showcased the work of those transnational actors. That is, the goal of this mixed-methods approach was to feature community voices in the form of narratives and to then visualize transnational actions from around the world. John W. Creswell and Viki L. Plano Clark state that a mixed-methods approach uses a combination of methods, research design, and philosophical orientations to collect and analyze qualitative and quantitative data rigorously in response to research questions. A mixed-methods approach, therefore, integrates two forms of data (quantitative and qualitative) and their results (how transnational networks function on a people-to-people level and how they function on a societal, cultural, and global level). I chose mixed-methods to provide space to cultivate reflexivity in data collection, analysis, and writing. In the following sections, I describe both of my methods as well as my strategies for data collection and analysis and end with limitations of the study and conclusion.

## Qualitative Research: Narrative Inquiry

Here, my focus was to understand the experiences of disaster responders who actively participated in community work during the Nepal earthquake and Hurricane Maria. To understand the community members' work and contributions, I conducted a narrative inquiry (See Appendix C for guiding questions) as this method provides a holistic view of social phenomena while ceding agency to the research participants so that they may narrate their own stories (Watkins and Gioia). It is important to represent the lived experiences of people who have contributed their time and energy to supporting others, not to mention the value such experiences have when conducting community-based research. Narrative inquiry allowed what Natasha N. Jones refers to as the "unique sensitivity to participants' epistemological and ontological perspectives by tapping into their lived experiences" ("Rhetorical Narratives" 327). With this in mind, I worked to listen to the in-depth description of my participants' experiences, gathered their stories, and analyzed their motivations and the work that they did for their community during the Nepal earthquake and Hurricane Maria.

As someone who experienced the Nepal earthquake, I have an emotional connection to my hometown and my own personal opinions as well as bias regarding the interpretation of the event and the global response. To overcome these challenges, I tried to rely on the eyewitness accounts of my participants, as well as objective research that was conducted on the event. While acknowledging my personal bias, I have tried to become as objective as possible to avoid interpreting my data based on my personal opinion. Instead, I did my best to allow my data to reveal the themes themselves. Puerto Rico was a completely new area for me. I wasn't part of the Puerto Rican community and had very limited in-depth knowledge of the cultures and histories of its communities. Moreover, I experienced a language barrier, since some of my interviewees spoke only Spanish. To understand the culture of the community, I allowed the participants to tell me their stories. Conversations with them about the social, cultural, political, and religious contexts of Puerto Rico helped me understand the communities. Moreover, as someone who is always concerned about Western researchers interpreting and imposing their definitions onto

Nepal and Nepali culture, I wanted to avoid conducting my research in ways that interpret Puerto Rico from an outsider's point of view. Recognizing that I am an outsider in their community, I again relied on my participants' narratives and tried to analyze those narratives as objectively as possible without any preconceived notions. While interpreting these interviews, I also made comparisons between two different countries and contexts. To make my comparison unbiased, I again went back to comparative rhetorics and the idea of self-reflexivity (Mao et al.). Comparative rhetorics offers a method for making comparisons between two different cultures, creating a common context by putting both cultures side by side and not making one superior to the other. While comparative rhetorics have mostly analyzed ancient texts, with the same grounding, I worked with very different data sets. Here, self-reflexivity allows researchers to think deeply about their methods and analyses and avoid imposing their personal understanding on the interpretation of the behaviors of the cultures they aren't a part of.

As part of this IRB-approved research, I interviewed 28 participants, of which 14 had experiences with the Nepal earthquake and 14 had experiences with Hurricane Maria. Some of the interviews were conducted via Skype. To find participants for this research, I searched publicly available social media profiles, reached out to potential participants, and relied on my contacts to recommend other possible contacts, thus using the snowball sampling method. Once I had gathered all of my contacts, I invited online and offline activists, government representatives, community leaders, community-based organizations, and members of the Nepali and Puerto Rican diaspora to the interview. All my participants had a direct involvement in performing networked activities, disaster relief work, and crisis communications work during the two disasters. They were activists, journalists, nongovernmental organization (NGO) workers, government representatives, students, teachers, and members of a diaspora. It was important to me to include women participants; thus, half of the participants were female and half were male.

The interviews were conducted in English, Nepali, and Spanish. In these interviews, which lasted 45 to 90 minutes each, my goal was to listen, record, and understand the narratives of the participant. Interviewing diverse individuals provided me with varied and unique perspectives on how disaster response was conducted from the official and unofficial sectors. The interviews provided the participants with a platform, and oftentimes, as they shared their stories, the interviews became intense and emotional, making it difficult for me to maintain the researcher and participant boundaries. Each interview became an informal sharing of stories, experiences, and the work that my participants did during the time of the disaster. All the recorded interviews were transcribed, and a qualitative data analysis was conducted via NVivo for Mac. NVivo is a qualitative data analysis application that allows for the scientific coding of interview-based research. I used NVivo because of its efficiency. NVivo provided me with a space to organize, store, and retrieve the qualitative data that I collected for my project. Moreover, NVivo provided me with data management, query, and visualization tools. As part of the IRB approval, I am not allowed to provide a name or a pseudonym for the participants. Using "participants" in the text that follows, however, should be seen as a failure to recognize their profound individual and collective humanity.

In making the methodological choice for this study, I carefully chose my participants who were part of the transnational crisis publics in order to highlight their work in supporting the communities that suffered through disaster in both Nepal and Puerto Rico. As such, all the participants had access to a phone, computer, and internet as well as language proficiency and educational abilities that helped them advocate on behalf of their communities. Highlighting their work is important for this research as they represent and provide alternative narratives of the marginalized community, their needs, and their suffering, which often were ignored by the governmental and big humanitarian actors. These participants, whom I call actors in this book, had access, privilege, and knowledge of using social media platforms and the power of challenging the status quo of the respective government and providing a more nuanced understanding of disaster-suffered communities. Hence, in this way, the project is limited because participants who were interviewed had an active role in disaster response through digital or nondigital means.

### Quantitative Research: Social Network Analysis

For my quantitative research, I used social network analysis (SNA) to study the formation and mobilization of networks among Twitter users from various countries during the Nepal earthquake and Hurricane Maria. SNA uses graphs and visualizations of networks to understand and analyze social phenomena (Borgatti and Everett;

Wasserman and Faust). My purpose for conducting SNA was limited to the following:

- Visualizing the transnational networks in terms of how actors from different countries relate to each other
- Comparing the visualizations of transnational networks during the Nepal earthquake and Hurricane Maria
- Understanding how the patterns of relations have affected disaster response efforts during the Nepal earthquake and Hurricane Maria

The SNA of Twitter data from the Nepal earthquake and Hurricane Maria helped me observe the various networks that formed during these two events and how people joined or left a social network on the basis of tasks to be accomplished, as well as their levels of interests, resources, and commitments. Stanley Wasserman and Katherine Faust define social networks as "a set of nodes (or network members) that are tied by one or more types of relations" (20). Social networks are usually studied on two levels—egocentric, where the network of individual actors is studied, and whole network, where all the actors (individual, community, and organizations) are studied together (Goswami et al. 3). Network analysis typically determines the presence and degree of connectedness among actors in terms of a variety of relationships, such as information, resource sharing, and emotional support (Goswami et al. 5). I thus had to choose the appropriate platform, the right tool, and, once I had those, I had to analyze the collected data.

While there are countless social media platforms that were used during both the Nepal earthquake and Hurricane Maria, choosing onc particular social media platform would narrow down the scope of research and make the study very specific. Twitter was one of the major platforms that people used during the two calamities. Moreover, Twitter users reveal considerably less private data, and their main activity is sending tweets, which is meant to be a public message and thus publicly available (Moffit). I therefore chose Twitter as my area of focus for understanding how it became a space for transnational interactions during the Nepal earthquake and Hurricane Maria because a) it has a representative population of users from around the world, b) it displays users' geo-locations, c) most of the data is public and easily accessible, d) the purchase of the historical tweets is easier when compared to other social media, and e) Twitter can provide a corpus of data (tweets) for analysis. I had also personally used Twitter during the Nepal earthquake, and I observed the activity related to Hurricane Maria on the platform. I was therefore familiar with Twitter as a space where people around the world would participate in disaster response.

After choosing Twitter as my social media platform, I decided to explore its data collection methods. Eventually, I decided to purchase data from Twitter's sister organization, Gnip; however, there were many processes that were associated with the data purchase. The first step in data collection was to identify an appropriate corpus of data. There were two different options: Historical Power Track and Full-Archive Search. Both options would provide publicly available tweets from March 2006 onward. A Historical Power Track would generate a data set containing tweets that were tweeted within ten-minute periods. From this option, one can limit their data set to the specific things they are looking for, such as dates, locations, hashtags, and keywords. Thus, because of this option's specificity, I chose the Historical Power Track data purchase.

For me to purchase the data, my case had to be approved. As determined by Gnip, a case explains a) the scope of my study, b) the purpose of my study, and c) the specific kinds of tweets I needed. The details of my explanation are in Appendix A. I have also included my contract with Twitter in Appendix B. Table 1.1 displays the choices I made when purchasing the data. Because I was trying to purchase the data from the Nepal earthquake and Hurricane Maria, I explored and identified various popular hashtags that were used during these two disasters. Then, I narrowed down the dates. The start date for the data was the day the event happened, and the end date was the eighth day after the event. Next, I narrowed down the locations from where I was purchasing the data. As shown in Table 1.1, the region for Nepal included Nepal, Asia, Europe, the United States, Latin America, and Australia, and the region for Puerto Rico was only Puerto Rico and the United States due to limitation of funding. The total number of tweets purchased was 36 million tweets from Nepal and 20 million tweets from Puerto Rico. Gnip delivered the data in a JavaScript Object Notation (JSON) format. The corpus of data consisted of a user's ID, screen name, location, protection (if a user's tweets are protected), verified status (some user accounts are verified by Twitter, which indicates that a Twitter account genuinely belongs to a notable user), followers, friends, listed (if users are listed in certain groups), favorites, status, reply, retweet, favorite, language, and timestamps.

**Table 1.1. Twitter Data Purchases**

| Location | Hashtags | Time Frame | Regions |
|---|---|---|---|
| Nepal | #NepalEarthquake, #earthquake, #QuakeNepal, #quakeNepal, #earthquakenepal, #EarthquakeNepal, #Pray4Nepal, #NepalQuake, #NepalEarthquakeRelief, #NepalQuakeRelief, #prayfornepal, #NepalRelief, #NepalRises | 4/24/15–5/1/15 | Nepal, Asia, Europe, US, Latin America, Australia |
| Puerto Rico | #Hurricane, #HurricaneMaria, #Relief, #PuertoRico #Boricua, #StayStrong, #ReliefEfforts, #PuertoRicoStrong, #PuertoRicoRelief, #UnitedForPuertoRico, #PuertoRicoWillRise, #Maria #PuertoRicoLoHaceMejor, #HuracanMaria, #UnidosPorPuertoRico, #PuertoRicoStrong, #Comfort4PuertoRico | 9/17/17–9/24/17 | Puerto Rico, USA |

After collecting the corpus of the Twitter data, I conducted the SNA. I only focused on finding out whether users from around the world created transnational connections via Twitter. I wanted to understand how people responded to disaster online during the first week of the two disasters, specifically analyzing connections made by using features such as reply or retweet. I asked Dr. Takahiro Yabe (a graduate student friend at that time and currently an assistant professor at New York University Tandon School of Engineering) to help me create graphs and visuals using the Python programming language based on what I specifically wanted to visualize. I regarded the actors' locations as a node, and the actors' replies and retweets as the relationship or connection between actors. I have not separated the replies and retweets in my data because I considered both to be actions that describe a connection. All the actors whose geolocation in the data was set to Nepal were counted as a part of the Nepal "node." The nodes from Nepal are connected to other nodes (e.g., United States, Australia, etc.) by replies and retweets. SNA also involves creating matrices, so I changed the JSON file of the Twitter data into matrices by creating weights, where the weight of each link corresponds to the number of replies and retweets that occurred among the countries.

Additionally, there was a limitation involved with the Twitter data I purchased as well as SNA. Due to budget limitations, I could purchase only a limited data set from both Nepal and Puerto Rico. The purchase of Twitter data also took me longer than expected. This delay limited my ability to engage with the data as much as I would have liked. Hence, I had to seek help from an expert to visualize the data quickly so I would be able to use it in my research. The data I purchased is only from a seven-day time frame; hence, due to the limited time frame and limitation of scope, the data reflects transnational connections created only within these seven days. As a result, my research was limited to looking at the initial disaster response; nevertheless, the limited data did allow me to answer my overall research question.

By gathering the experiences of ordinary people who have been actively involved in relief and rescue during these two catastrophic events, I aimed to not only highlight individual experiences but also to explore the social, cultural, and familial narratives within which individuals' experiences are constituted, shaped, expressed, and enacted (Clandinin; N. N. Jones). Likewise, the quantitative data helped me in creating visual representations of the social relations, which I present in the following chapters. These representations offer a broader picture of the networks that formed during and after the Nepal earthquake and Hurricane Maria that revealed social relationship among Twitter users during these two disasters. With these methods, in this book, I attempt to understand the rhetoric of disaster in the globalized world, via an in-depth understanding of the operation of transnational assemblages during a disaster. I used a narrative approach to recognize my positionality as an international researcher. Using a mixed-methods approach allowed me to identify some interesting results which help in understanding both the micro- and macro-levels of disaster response. A mixed-methods approach was also ideal for answering the research questions with which I began this study.

## CONCLUSION

Transnational assemblages during a disaster create a moment where people from all around the world can come and participate. The rhetoric of disaster within such assemblages creates space for people to discuss racial, caste-based, geography-based injustices and unequal distribution of resources in addition to creating pressure on the formal entities, like the government, to act. While it may not resolve all the deep-down societal issues, such a rhetorical moment helps to create awareness of root causes and systemic oppressions. The formation of transnational assemblages during a disaster is inevitable, and those assemblages help in disaster recovery. When we ground crisis communication in intersectionality and social justice, it will help us to contextualize information based on the local context where there are many different types of intersections. Likewise, the work of actors who emerge during a disaster is dynamic and powerful. I will further elaborate on this in the next two chapters and showcase how identifying those actors and their assemblages might help in supporting the most marginalized and vulnerable communities. Understanding the work of the actors within their transnational assemblages will allow us to focus on marginalized communities suffering through systemic oppressions. Furthermore, this will showcase a path to advocacy.

This chapter covered the discourse surrounding technology, rhetorics, and disaster by locating disaster and networks in rhetorical theory and creating space to discuss how we can rethink the rhetoric of disaster and how such rethinking supports TPC, rhetorical scholars, and practitioners. I extended the theoretical framework of transnational assemblages and showcased how such expansion is required to implement ethical and socially just disaster response. With this expansion, my hope is that we as scholars continue to study disaster with a grounding in social justice and create a platform where we can discuss how our scholarship can support marginalized voices across the globe. In the following chapters, I will showcase the actual work of the various transnational assemblages and actors during the Nepal earthquake and Hurricane Maria and how they have created rhetoric of disaster via transnational assemblages that allowed them to support their communities suffering through these two catastrophic crises.

# 2

## Non-Western Disaster Response during the April 25, 2015, Nepal Earthquake

On the day of the earthquake, I was in the middle of an early history workshop taking place in Patan. There were 35 of us on the first floor of an old building. When the earthquake struck, all of us were able to get out of the building relatively unscathed. Some of us had bruises, but we were lucky that the building had remained intact. I was surprised at how quickly we were able to get out of the building. We went to find an open space. Within the first ten minutes after the earthquake, I got a call from a friend in Delhi. I was surprised that the phones were working, as I had been trying to reach my parents but wasn't able to do so. (I was eventually able to reach my parents, and they were okay.) I received another call from the producer of a news channel whom I had met some time ago. He asked me if I could do a piece on the earthquake. I went live on their channel within the first 20 minutes after the earth had stopped shaking. At that time, the helicopters had already started to fly. While I was fielding phone calls and messages, some people from our group decided that they wanted to go and see if they could help anyone. We were just trying to make sure that everyone was okay. I received photos on Viber depicting the destruction that occurred across Nepal, and I became very upset. The photos of the damage also started to circulate on Facebook and Instagram. The information was spreading very quickly through both social media and visual communication.

The next day, some of my friends and my brother felt the urge to do something. They had just taken their first-aid training courses, and they felt that they could offer their skills and knowledge to help those in need. We made a post on Facebook announcing that our meeting would be at a given place and

> that anyone who was interested could join us. In the following days, more and more people who shared our desire to help others joined our meetings, making our efforts a huge success. Hundreds of people started showing up on any given day. There was a massive crowd. So many people had joined our group that, for one day, we could not control the crowd anymore. We eventually had to wonder how we could manage and organize these crowds, but what was certain from the very first day that we assembled this group was that we wanted to create a space so that people who felt compelled to help could do so. We wanted to gather, make plans, and see what we could do to make everyone's recovery a little easier. We discussed the needs of the people and how we could address those needs. We also started to fundraise thanks to two of my friends. One friend was based in New York (USA), and the other friend was based in Belgium. Both of them set up a fundraising platform.
>
> – Participant, Nepal

On April 25, 2015, Nepalis experienced one of the biggest disasters in nearly a century. This disaster not only brought devastation to the nation, but also created a humanitarian crisis. Nepal is a small, landlocked country that is very prone to natural disasters. The nation had not experienced such a large earthquake since the 1920s. It was predicted that a big tremor would eventually strike Nepal, though no one knew when. The earthquake that struck in 2015 had a 7.5 magnitude, a convulsion that rattled 14 districts, including that of my hometown, Kathmandu. This disaster killed 8,856 people and injured 22,309. The earthquake created chaos by bringing life to a standstill and by generating a large humanitarian crisis. Many global actors, including various countries, organizations, communities, and individuals, turned their attention to this event. Nepal Flash Appeal for the response to the Nepal Earthquake released by the United Nations reported that 4.2 million people including 1.7 million children required health, water, sanitation, and hygiene related support. Fortunately, the earthquake happened at a time when Nepal was adapting to the current digital age. A section of educated, technology-savvy Nepali people in Nepal and beyond thus had an active presence on the social web. This resulted in a wider engagement with the global actors that were involved in disaster response efforts and in supporting the suffering Nepali communities.

Within three days of the earthquake, the United Nations (UN) sent out a flash appeal to raise 422 million US dollars to meet the needs of countless suffering Nepalis. Out of the total amount of money requested, 48 percent was requested specifically for health, hygiene, and food security ("Nepal Flash Appeal"). This request was publicized using social media channels, including the UN website. Mark Zuckerberg, the CEO of Facebook, also set up a fundraiser to help people affected by the earthquake. One week after the earthquake, Zuckerberg, via his Facebook page, announced that "more than 750,000 people from around the world gave over $15 million to the International Medical Corps relief efforts, and Facebook donated an additional $2 million on top of that to local recovery efforts." Jennifer Sano-Franchini argues that "Facebook took up this cause [earthquake], collecting more than $15 million in donations and deploying its safety check feature to help indicate whom among Facebook users in Nepal were 'safe' in the midst of the national crisis" (395). With this generous support pouring in from all around the world, the UN reported that "103,686 injured people received treatment, including 2,088 who had undergone major surgeries, and 26,160 who had received psychosocial support in 14 districts" ("Nepal Flash Appeal"). However, as CNN reported, "[i]n the countryside, not too far from the quake's epicenter, mountain villages are cut off from almost everything. Landslides block the roads and no significant aid is on the way" ("Nepal Earthquake: Mountain Villagers"). The most marginalized groups in Nepal suffered the most, as is the case everywhere.

I experienced the earthquake and witnessed the devastation that it brought firsthand. I also became a part of the disaster response effort in the capacity of a journalist, communications practitioner. During 2015, mobile and internet technologies were not new to the Nepali people. Many were familiar with assorted technologies, including various digital platforms such as Facebook, Twitter, Instagram, and blogging. Social media platforms became a space where global interactions could happen among the Nepalis and the international communities who wanted to help and support the Nepalis. Immediately following the earthquake, the Nepalis on Twitter mobilized themselves in responding to the disaster by serving their communities. I argue that this mobilization of local and transnational Nepali communities (who interacted, worked with non-Nepalis communities) is a powerful representation of what the non-Western disaster response looks like, a response that differs from the very individualistic Western response and focuses on social justice. In effect, during the aftermath of the earthquake, Nepalis in Nepal, the Nepali diaspora, and international communities and organizations became interconnected through a complex transnational assemblage.

Such assemblages also demonstrated that responding to such a large-scale disaster requires multisectoral coalitional actions to address historic injustices. Karma Chávez suggests that the term *coalition* embodies multiple meanings based on various social and political contexts. In the case of disaster, such coalitions are formed spontaneously as the disaster demands urgency of response to save lives. Similarly, coalitions can also be spaces where multiple parties can engage, but often require constant work if that coalition were to endure (Chávez). As I described previously, these transnational assemblages are coalitional networks created among people across national boundaries and are formed by affective interactions mediated via digital media. Within these transnational assemblages, various actors circulate information, data, and knowledge across the border by mobilizing cross-cultural power, language, resources, and people (Hesford and Schell; Potts; Baniya and Potts; Baniya and Chen). As Rebecca Walton, Kristen Moore, and Natasha Jones posit, oppressions cannot be combated alone, which is why joining coalitions, building genuine allyships, and working toward a sustainable practice of activism are necessary and required specifically in the context of a large-scale disaster.

The power of such transnational assemblages to confront injustices was showcased during the Nepal earthquake via *swa-byabasthapan*. I argue that this concept in Nepal, loosely translated as "self-management," was the non-Western way of building coalitions via transnational assemblages to challenge the traditional disaster response by making such response accessible to marginalized publics. Understanding the formation of transnational assemblages and the coalition building that occurs within those assemblages to resist catastrophic disasters will help in appreciating how people help themselves and their communities in times of chaos. To achieve this understanding, I find it necessary to highlight the ignored survival practices of marginalized communities who have navigated oppressive systems to restore peace and stability in their communities. Highlighting these survival practices that are both local and transnational will help in building/

strengthening community resilience and preparing for eventual future disasters with a grounding of social justice.

In the detailed case study which follows, I provide an overview of how Nepalis and global actors responded to this disaster within social media spaces and physical communities. The results I present are based on 14 interviews I conducted with the Nepalis and non-Nepalis who contributed to disaster relief efforts during the Nepal earthquake, and the social network analysis of the Twitter data collected from the first week after the earthquake. I specifically focus on articulating how the local actors collaborated, challenged, and resisted the offical response with their own local, non-Western ways of knowledge-making during the disaster. I believe my findings will demonstrate that transnational assemblages conduct activism and engagement in disaster response that leads to the discovery and accentuation of social justice issues within marginalized spaces that may otherwise remain hidden. Such a revelation is largely made possible by using assorted internet-based technologies and social media platforms. As such, as I introduce the non-Western ways of disaster response grounded in *swa-byabasthapan*, I argue that, while larger formal global disaster response happens, various local contexts and knowledge gets ignored, resulting in the marginalization of vulnerable communities.

## TRANSNATIONAL ASSEMBLAGES AS NON-WESTERN DISASTER RESPONSE STRATEGIES

In the aftermath of the Nepal earthquake, the activists representing global communities from transnational spaces responded to the calamity by going beyond the state-oriented or formal organizations' disaster response protocols that often left many communities ignored. In fact, the efforts of unofficial actors resulted in quick actions that arose from the establishment of coalitions via networked collaborations supported by digital platforms. These quick actions, in turn, served Nepali communities residing in remote areas who are marginalized and vulnerable due to their gender, caste, education, and geographical locations, and who would have otherwise been overlooked by the government or because events like landslides and road blockages hindered delivery of aid. The earthquake in Nepal came at a time when Nepal was already vulnerable due to its own concurrent issues of small-scale disasters, social discrimination, political turmoil, and geopolitics. For example, soon after the Nepal earthquake there was a border blockade orchestrated by India which the Nepali prime minister at that time described as "more inhumane than war" ("Nepal Border Blockade"). However, India has vehemently denied orchestrating the standoff that created another level of crisis in Nepal ("Nepal Border Blockade").

Even though Nepal has eradicated the caste system and has changed a lot of rules and regulations on gender, there are still people, particularly women, who are on the margins, specifically those who belong to Madehsi and Dalit communities. While in terms of representation there are women who fill leadership seats, they are still from privileged caste groups. Kalpana Jha argues that "women [in Nepal] with intersectional identities still have a minimal presence in all spheres of public and private institutions with Madhesi and Dalit women almost nonexistent in most leadership positions" (n.p.). And certain communities are always at a disadvantage because of race, caste, gender, and the geographical location where they reside. In the aftermath of the earthquake, those disadvantages were more apparent than ever. Nearly two months after the Nepal earthquake, Amnesty International's Asia Pacific director said in a briefing that "survivors report that in some communities the aid effort has been politically manipulated. Those with muscle—political connections—end up claiming desperately needed supplies meant for everyone" ("Nepal: End"). Unfortunately, this was a very common practice post-Nepal earthquake which often the transnational assemblages criticized publicly as they acted to support the communities in need.

Furthermore, like other countries' governments, there was no way the Nepali government was prepared for such a large-scale disaster. Nepal does have a lot of international support from the world's humanitarian organizations, like the United Nations, the European Union, the Red Cross, and Care International, among others. These organizations are criticized time and again for lack of work; however, they are/were still better equipped to handle disasters. Unfortunately, due to bureaucracy and strict protocols, these organizations ended up not being able to handle the entirety of the Nepal community's needs in the wake of the earthquake. That is because one organization or entity can never handle the aftereffects of such a catastrophic disaster, hence, the requirement of transnational assemblages. Most of the time, the Western disaster response comes in the form of large amounts of money or volunteers from all over the world. Often, disaster response leaders have little or no context of the

Nepal communities. Such disaster response is also launched by official organizations such as governments that have bureaucratic protocols to follow. In the case of Nepal, then, such a Western disaster response was available but was not fulfilling the needs of the entire community. The Western-centric organizational approach, challenged by language and cultural differences, hindered the disaster response process.

In the wake of the Nepal earthquake, then, many of the official transnational organizational networks that were designed to help in organizing larger-scale disaster response efforts were either influenced by Western disaster practices or, like the government, were too overwhelmed. The Nepali government organized a "donor conference," where leaders from differing countries pledged monetary assistance to Nepal to respond to the earthquake. Similarly, networks of international nongovernmental/humanitarian organizations, like the United Nations, the European Union, and the Red Cross, also helped in the disaster response efforts. When I interviewed my research participants, nine of them noted that they had been a part of official networks that allowed them to become involved in disaster response. A participant who represents a network of international humanitarian organizations working in Nepal shared that, soon after the earthquake, there was an upsurge in international organizations who came to Nepal to support Nepali communities. She recounts the following:

> I think it [disaster response] was from 36 countries altogether. There are a lot of members in our country too. Some are from America and other places. Everybody from all over the world has done at least something from their side. Everybody helped and we also collected some amount of money from members. (Participant from Nepal)

As the participant noted, many organizations from around the world came to Nepal to provide support. During the earthquake, the Nepal government eased governmental policies and welcomed both smaller and larger organizations that offered aid and support to Nepalis. Sadly, however, the support coming from these organizations was often very haphazard and not well maintained. Other issues that these organizations encountered involved cultural, language, and contextual differences. Thus, even though a lot of organizations came together to "support" the suffering Nepali communities, they presented their resources without having community knowledge, which turned out to be a major issue. A lack of community knowledge combined with the government's relief mismanagement would have resulted in many communities never receiving the aid they desperately needed. However, they had an alternative: the transnational assemblages.

The alternative, grassroots-level disaster response performed by individuals within transnational assemblages who did not wait for the government or any official organizations for help in the context of the Nepal earthquake could be considered the "non-Western" response. The non-Western disaster response is grounded in *swa-byabasthapan*, which allows the disaster responders—whose actions are gauged by the sense of collaborative actions necessary to address the injustices these individual communities must face—to understand the community and its needs. This effort is typically localized and acts as an alternative way of responding to a disaster. The non-Western disaster response praxis allows for immediate actions that are not restricted by formal protocols. It allows individual actors to support each other throughout the disaster, network across the diasporic communities, and decentralize aid. With the emergence of transnational assemblages within local areas, online spaces, and beyond where people meet in alternative spaces to discuss disaster response efforts, this way of disaster response provides immediate relief to the communities that the government and other organizations did not reach. This response is not influenced by the official organizations' protocols, however; it is self-managed. The non-Western ways of disaster response are instead localized in the community while their networks are established within transnational communities composed of people who might be affected by the disaster, might be less affected by the immediate consequences of the disaster, or might not be affected at all (e.g., residing in other countries).

Aside from providing aid to marginalized communities, the Nepalis' transnational assemblages also worked toward revealing the unethical practices of the government, media, and the larger humanitarian organizations by bringing to light the irregularities and misconduct these entities took part in when they should have been responding to the disaster. One of the major issues identified by Nepali participants was that the government and humanitarian organizations were too focused on their official protocols and not on the lives of people. They were seen by my participants as more invested in writing reports than organizing relief. Even the discourses related to the disaster were exposed for their unjust representation by highlighting the difference between what was said and what was happening. For instance, Nepali activists on Twitter revealed that the United Nations World Food Program distributed rotten food to marginalized communities ("WFP to Destroy"). This issue was denied by the WFP; however, there was photographic evidence that was made public on Twitter which told otherwise. While disaster response might have been done in good faith, such negligence and distribution of the rotten food was unacceptable.

Similarly, activists launched a hashtag trend against the Indian media, which was making inadequate and inaccurate reports regarding the Nepal earthquake. As reported by BBC News, "A reporter seized a wounded survivor and paraded her in front of the cameras rather than putting some cloth to stop the bleeding . . . . Yet another kept asking rescue workers what technology they were using at work. In a quake-hit village, a reporter worked up a veritable hysteria, asking affected villagers what their government was actually doing for them" ("Why is Indian Media"). In response to such inhumane behavior showcased by the Indian media outlets, these transnational assemblage members called out Indian media. Hence, the Nepali community went against these practices with the hashtag #GoHomeIndianMedia (see Figures 2.1 and 2.2). This hashtag was supported by several communities, such as those in Nepal, India, and Pakistan ("Why is Indian Media"). Non-Western disaster response in the context of Nepal saw the public acting against the traditional norms and holding organizations accountable for what they were communicating and what they were doing in the community. The work of transnational assemblages was important because it highlighted the injustices that were brought about by a lack of proper disaster response or inhumane reporting. By tackling such injustices, the disaster responders and activists within their own spaces, localities, and beyond created transnational coalitional networks or assemblages. These networked actions became a communal force that did not wait for formal mechanisms to respond to the disaster but instead spontaneously fundraised, gathered resources, and formulated disaster management plans and conducted aid-delivery.

Figure 2.1. A tweet by Suchana, which started the conversation on #GoHomeIndianMedia.

Figure 2.2. Another tweet by Prasanna KC adding to the conversation with more retweets and likes.

The individuals in transnational assemblages who were disaster responders and activists helped tremendously in responding to the earthquake by also launching various small-scale efforts. This work was carried out on assorted internet-based platforms such as Google Docs, Twitter, WhatsApp, and Facebook Messenger. These transnational assemblages had local networks and connections, and were composed of individuals who were sharing information, news, and requests for resources. Eileen Schell believes that global communities form informal networks of activists across borders to act and respond to specific social, economic, and political issues such as "environment, labor, human rights, human trafficking, and global trade policies" (589). In collaborating and participating, the activists' network becomes stronger and stabilizes as the actors contribute their content, curate information, and mobilize others in their network to disseminate knowledge effectively and efficiently (Dadas; Potts). One participant, for example, mentioned that their friends at home and abroad sent them relief materials such as tarpaulins, food, and water supplies. Once the participant received these supplies, they and their network delivered the goods by motorbike to rural places that the government and other international organizations had not reached as aid-delivery trucks or vans couldn't go due to road conditions. The activists' spontaneous actions are powered by the speed of the internet in circulating content, information, issue, and affect (Appadurai). In my participant's case, their network of friends who sent relief materials became aware of the earthquake's devastation thanks to the information posted on the social media platforms they used. Their friends acted because of their emotional and affective reactions to the information shared and posted online. The affective attunement enabled through digital media presents a way for diverse publics to be part of and emotionally align with the movement and happening (Papacharissi; Yam).

Disaster responders of the Nepal earthquake did not only use digital platforms to communicate, but they also created innovative technologies to gather disaster response data and coordinate relief efforts. One participant shared that they engaged in curating a web-based information platform for the government which later became the national disaster-based information website for Nepal. The government website was launched within a couple of days of the earthquake. Another participant shared that, due to the volume of volunteers and the need for disaster relief, they created their own web-based platform to match volunteers with the communities in need. They felt the need to do this because the official government website could not handle the sheer volume of traffic on its own and the government was overwhelmed. There were also tech-savvy activists in Nepal with organizations like Kathmandu Living Labs or Code for Nepal who created interactive maps by gathering data and information from the communities on the ground, an effort that helped hundreds of volunteers organize disaster response and which the government was unable to achieve as efficiently. Disaster responders and activists thus found new and innovative technological solutions to manage disaster response via proper data collection and management (Potts). These digital tools were created because other tools were not functioning to meet the requirements of the context, time, and community needs. The notion of not relying on traditional, official platforms to get the job done in times of a disaster is therefore one aspect of the non-Western disaster response where a lot of participants performed *swa-byabasthapan* to address the current needs of the community.

The Nepali diaspora along with the global community also played a significant role in conducting transnational disaster response by connecting to the local communities and engaging their communities abroad. Participants from the Nepali diaspora recounted that social media provided them with an easier means to connect to their communities back home, which in turn allowed them to organize their activism. The diasporic communities were not only connecting to their loved ones, they were also connecting to various other transcultural communities in need by establishing partnerships with local disaster responders. The Nepali communities around the globe organized their counter-public enclaves by sharing diverse embodiments such as oratorical, material, visual, or performative ones, which Chávez recognizes as the center of a social movement and, in this case, transnational activism. The sharing of data, information, and pictures on social media challenged traditional communication systems and created transnational assemblages where people from transnational communities could come together to respond to a disaster. These coalitional networks existed in contrast to the formal entities, like the government or national and international humanitarian organizations. They reached the communities that were ignored by the formal disaster responders. This form of disaster response showcases the diasporic communities' rhetorical practices of creating, curating, and circulating materials and discourses online as well as assembling disaster responders on the ground (Z.Wang).

As discussed earlier, disaster creates feelings of urgency and immediacy, leading to affective interactions among the people who are suffering and the people who are observing that suffering online. Humans use their senses, feelings, and emotions to react to worldwide calamities through non-human objects such as phones, computers, and buildings because they all coexist and are networked within the assemblage itself. The affective reactions, the sense of community in the people experiencing a crisis, whether physically or emotionally, motivate them to connect to others via assorted digital means, further helping to create transnational assemblages via coalitional actions and spontaneous reactions (Papacharissi; Yam). My participants stated that after the disaster, they were motivated to perform spontaneous actions to save lives, serve communities in need, and reach out to ask for help, creating their own transnational assemblages. The affective response in a disaster is spontaneous, as participants have noted in their narratives, because a post-crisis situation is a perfect time to act and help the community that needs instant support. Participants believed that their actions were oriented toward immediate relief and rescue to help in saving the lives of the people who were suffering.

For a non-Western community, this sense of supporting your neighbor or community is not new. These sentiments are grounded in the daily life praxis that is filled with various rituals and festivals that require the community to be together to celebrate, perform, and support each other. Such rituals allow people to be a part of the community and maintain their relationships, ties, and networks. Because of this deeply rooted sense of community, when the Nepal earthquake happened, there was this reliance on local efforts as opposed to the efforts of official organizations. (Here it is important to also note that many Nepalis do not live in Nepal as there is a lot of migration to the Gulf countries and to the United States, United Kingdom, and Australia, among others.) The transnational assemblages that spontaneously emerged in response to the earthquake upheld the non-Western sentiment of community which is part of the Nepali identity despite actors being far from home or the love and dedication to Nepal, a sentiment that my participants all seemed to share. This identity created an opportunity for people affected by the catastrophe to depend on the transnational assemblages that prioritized their needs. My participants confirmed that they would rather depend on their networks of friends, family members, or even strangers whom they met online to conduct disaster response as opposed to entrusting official entities with that task. The activists and disaster responders on the ground, therefore, depended on the transnational assemblages formed via diasporic networks involving people from multiple countries, nationalities, communities, and transcultural contexts. These transnational activists are affectively connected with less emphasis on personal differences and an increase in conformity in belief that they are working for the community (Delanda). This change in priorities leads toward collaboration as everyone in the assembly has a shared mission of supporting communities in need. Community gathering and supporting each other are therefore embedded in the non-Western culture.

Transnational assemblages were formed via networked connections and communications in the aftermath of the earthquake. The social web helped actors create, enhance, and maintain those connections. All 14 participants revealed their dependencies on interpersonal networks, professional networks, and networks created via the social web. Collectively, the participants stated that they a) reached out to their family, friends, and friends of friends; b) instituted professional networked participation through the organizations that they were a part of; c) established stronger networks through the use of social media; d) reached out to their respective diaspora network; and e) expanded networks by joining or leaving the various disaster relief groups. The formation of the diverse kinds of networks helped Nepal respond to the calamity in a quicker and more efficient manner.

Many of the networks that formed on social media platforms in the wake of the Nepal earthquake were motivated by the Nepali people's sense of community, as discussed above, particularly their affective response toward the situation of disaster. From what I could gather, my participants described similar experiences as they confronted the calamity. Some of them, for example, were physically present in Nepal when the earthquake struck; others, on the other hand, were far away from their home country. What united the two was the way they experienced the disaster on the social web and their willingness to join a community that worked to support their home country or their local town. Actors, therefore, experienced a common sentiment of fear, which evolved into a desire and a drive to be involved in spontaneous actions. By allowing actors to spontaneously respond to a disaster, the social web provides a platform for people to quickly organize their efforts. A participant shared the following:

> It was because that [disaster response] was very immediate at that time. Like, you would post one thing on the internet, on Facebook, and they [friends] would reach out to me. And then we would carry it [disaster response] from there. So, that was very instant. If you had a tarp at home, you would go, just . . . bring it [to someone who needed it]. (Participant from Nepal)

Similarly, another participant noted:

> For example, if a man is trapped . . . nearby, people did not wait for the government, they immediately went there and pulled

him out to save his life whether they were experts or not. (Participant from Nepal)

In these narratives, we see three common themes: urgency, using available means of communication, and acting immediately without waiting for the government. Participants used their Facebook accounts to bring attention to the dire situation, to request help, and to act instantly, thus motivating others who read the distraught status to become involved. The spontaneous actions that led to the affective response were mediated via social media platforms, which resulted in a networked and collective response. The desire to act immediately further helped in the formation of smaller assemblages that responded to the disaster. Transnational assemblages created via social media allowed the affective reactions to develop into a very substantive disaster response effort. These affective reactions are based on the sentiment of being Nepali or part of the Nepali community, which is deeply rooted within non-Western values of care and community support. These feelings and emotions are magnified during a time of disaster thanks to social media, where such feelings of care, community need, and motivations are shared and amplified. These values are non-Western with a sense of grounding within Nepali culture, traditional values, and/or caring for the Nepali community.

All the participants also demonstrated a sense of commitment toward their community that led them to create, be part of, or even leave, transnational assemblages. This joining or forming of informal networks during the disaster was supported by technology. Participants suggested that the reason why they would leave an assemblage was because they kept a focus on specific communities and its needs. If the assemblage got too big, they worried that the community's needs would not be satisfied, thus they would split off into smaller assemblages so that they could divide the work and so that they could support more communities. A prime example of this phenomenon can be found in one of my participant's experiences:

> Then we decided we were just an emergency responder, so we were not going to do long-term recruiting, we were only doing it in terms of immediate relief and emergency relief. The tarps were only temporary relief. It lasted a month, I guess. Before the second earthquake came, we were going to wrap up all these. But then we continued it for another two weeks. (Participant from Nepal)

In this narrative, we can see how the participant shared how they had been emergency responders but now their self-organizing efforts needed to come to an end. They had created communities that worked within their transnational assemblages. And, as the participant shares, there was a moment when they had to pause as they were only meant to do emergency response. While this assemblage came into existence and kept on growing, as the participants shared, there were some who would later decide to leave the network, or in this case, the network ceased to exist, while participants moved to other roles. Sometimes, the people who left the network would form their own separate disaster relief groups, their own smaller assemblages. For instance, another participant recounted that they first went to the Yellow House, a gathering space, as a volunteer to offer their support, but since there was a massive turnout and a lot of people were already involved, they decided to create their own relief group that focused specifically on helping the communities in Rasuwa, one of the worst-hit districts. This demonstrates how the informal transnational assemblages started to grow laterally and organically. What's more, these assemblages also started to reach beyond Nepal's borders and beyond the Nepali diaspora. A participant shared:

> We realized in less than one day that the issue was not money at that time because the Nepali people from abroad, and . . . foreigners who loved Nepal, were raising funds within two or three days. (Participant from Nepal)

This narrative suggests that people in Nepal were not networking exclusively among each other within the vicinity of their own country or region, but they were creating connections beyond their county's borders. Such a realization comforted many Nepalis who realized that the government would not come to their aid. Thus, the sense of commitment toward the community helped the participants and other Nepali people connect with those who felt similarly, working together to respond to the crisis without waiting for government aid that would never come. The Nepali people's resolve to serve and help themselves led to holding space in which new "articulations were being forged[, thus] constituting a new assemblage or territory" (Slack and Wise 158). This communal reliance is yet another component of the non-Western praxis.

As we can see, there is a lot of *swa-byabasthapan*, which I argue is a survival praxis of the non-Western communities as they need to self-organize and manage to get out of the situation of disaster. We saw this in examples among the Nepalis within Nepal and abroad. Like a lot of participants mentioned, money wasn't a problem—it was coming from all over the world—and human resources weren't a problem, as the transnational assemblages were already in action. The narratives also share a communal practice and a sense that I am alive, or I am a Nepali, and I need to support my community when they are in need. Moreover, this disaster response also acts as a resistance against the governmental practice as well as the Western practice.

## VISUALIZATION OF TRANSNATIONAL ASSEMBLAGES DURING THE NEPAL EARTHQUAKE

While the interviews provided in-depth stories of people who were actively working during the disaster, a social network analysis (SNA) of the Twitter data set allowed me to track networks across the world. This large quantitative data set supported the stories and amplified actors' experiences, visually portraying how people like my participants were engaged in disaster response efforts for Nepal across the world. Such actions were mobilized when larger transnational networks, which had their own affordances, formed. The participants in my study regularly stated that responding to the Nepal earthquake challenged them to communicate beyond language and cultural barriers. In going beyond those barriers, the participants' flexibility, and social media, made communications easier and more accessible, especially since most of them used the English language. Because the transnational assemblages were comprised of people in different locations and time zones, the work distribution was adjusted according to those diverse conditions. The SNA can portray such interactions, showcasing how these networks were formed and tracking the networks as they evolved over time. It is then possible to analyze these networks and their strength in organizing disaster relief efforts. Jordan Frith argues that "by drawing from SNA to map and conceptualize the social networks in which technical communicators operate, researchers will be able to understand the roles technical communicators play in organizations, the multiple audiences as they connect" (289). SNA helped in contextualizing the networks that transnational assemblages were part of as they connect to multiple audiences, organizations by performing communication-related tasks such as sharing information during the earthquake.

SNA in the study of technical and professional communication (TPC) can help in theorizing how information flows within a network, recognizing the principal actors in the network, and tracking how the network is mobilized when disseminating information. These relationships are based on individual relationships, organizational relationships, formal and information relationships, and ad hoc relationships. Such relationships are developed via shared interests or affective ties, which are based on network members' feelings toward one another or cognitive awareness (Borgatti; Papacharissi; Scott and Carrington). As such, SNA helps us conceptualize how transnational networks are formed, how people communicate across physical borders, and what roles users, organizations, and governments play in curating information online during a disaster event. SNA visually represents the relationships between points, or nodes, in a network. In the case of a disaster, the nodes in SNA represent actors, while the lines that connect the nodes represent the actors' interactions with each other. The SNA of the Nepal earthquake in Figure 2.3 represents the network formation on Twitter among the users from various countries and continents.

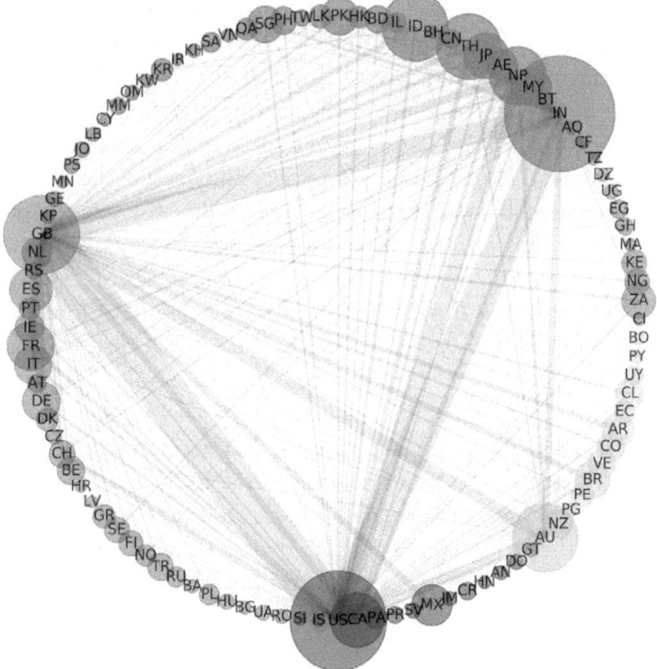


Figure 2.3. SNA among the users residing in various countries in the world during the Nepal earthquake.

In Figure 2.3, the larger nodes represent Asia (red), Africa (green), South America (light blue), Oceania (yellow), North America (purple), and Europe (dark blue). The smaller nodes represent the countries within these continents. The thickness of the lines connecting the nodes represents the strength of the relationships among the nodes. The thicker the lines, the stronger the ties and relationships among users residing in these countries.

As Figure 2.3 demonstrates, there were three prominent network clusters during the Nepal earthquake: Europe-Asia-North America, North America-Asia-Oceania, and Oceania-Europe-Asia. As shown in the figure, the strongest of these three networks was the Europe-Asia-North America network. This means that there was a higher frequency of replies and retweets among actors in this network. The other two major networks (North America-Asia-Oceania and Oceania-Europe-Asia) also revealed stronger relationships based on reply and retweet frequency. Ties among African and Latin American countries were weaker. One reason for such a weak relationship is due to less of a Nepali presence and weaker diplomatic partnerships in African and Latin American countries. Regardless, we can still notice that people tweeted, retweeted, or replied to posts involving the Nepal earthquake from all around the world.

The formation of strong networks was likely the result of three main factors: a) the European, Australian, and US governments and NGOs' investment in Nepal; b) the presence of Nepali populations in these continents; and c) various trade and economic relationships within the countries. All these countries, mainly the UK, US, and Australia, have a stronger connection to Nepal in terms of diplomacy, migration networks, and investment in developmental work in Nepal. However, on a more granular level, these stronger connections are made by the people from the transcultural communities (both Nepalis and non-Nepalis within Nepal and abroad). The visual representation of the relationships Nepal had with actors from other countries further confirms that transnational assemblages during a disaster operate across time zones, locations, and nationalities by creating their own smaller workspaces and territories, and this goes beyond the geopolitics.

An example of such a transnational assemblage is that of The Himalayan Disaster Relief Volunteer Group, which one of my participants founded. The Himalayan Disaster Relief Volunteer Group was formed right after the Nepal earthquake, and it was composed of numerous Nepalis and nationals from other countries. This come-as-you-like group would gather, share information, and do whatever the community needed them to do. While some of the members were fundraising and creating connections outside of Nepal, there were volunteers on the ground distributing relief materials to the people affected by the crisis. The Himalayan Disaster Relief Volunteer Group's report, shared openly (see Figure 2.4), depicts the places and communities that they were able to serve during the calamity. This visual showcases how disaster response was happening. While the visualization of SNA showcases how larger networks were formed, this visual shows ground work and action that was happening while funds were raised outside Nepal and were sent for disaster response mobilizations.

The reach represented by Figure 2.4 would not have been possible had the Nepali community on the ground not formed its relations outside of Nepal. As many participants mentioned, and the Himalayan Disaster Relief Volunteer Group leader expressly shared, there were two countries where fundraising was being organized simultaneously: the USA (North America) and Belgium (Europe).

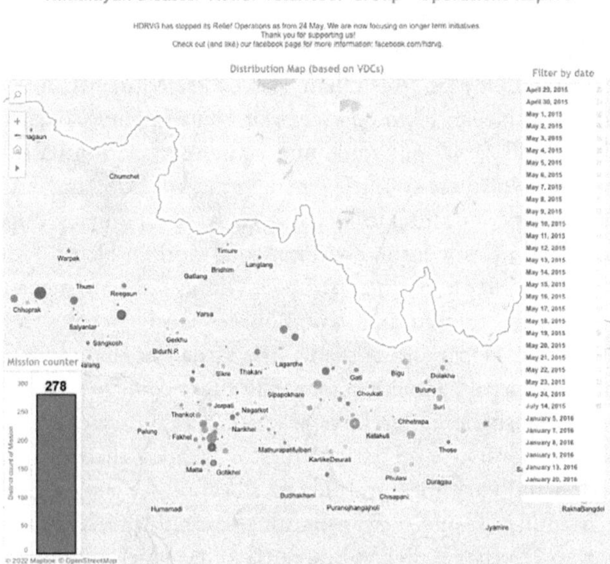


Figure 2.4. Map of relief distribution completed by The Himalayan Disaster Relief Volunteer Group.

We can see that those connections might be very macro level, but the larger networks of connections made sure that disaster response was happening on the ground, and Figure 2.4 showcases such possibilities of the work of transnational assemblages.

## AGAINST THE DOMINANT NARRATIVES: TRANSNATIONAL ASSEMBLAGES IN ACTION

The previous visualization of transnational assemblage networks showcases the connections that were created on social media during the Nepal earthquake. One can see how there are stronger relationships among actual people who reside in these various countries. With this visualization of the larger data and very granular stories of *swa-byabasthapan*, we can argue that social media during the Nepal earthquake became a multifaceted platform for digital activism. Activists used these platforms against the dominant narratives that have worked to suppress minority voices and create their own space for discussing and challenging injustices. This kind of activism was not only limited to the use of social media, but it also involved technological innovations such as web-based and phone-based applications, geographic information system (GIS) maps, and a supply chain management apparatus for volunteers and relief supplies. Activists during and after the disaster emerged as a rhizome, or a source (Deleuze and Guattari), that connected with other activists who were part of an existing assemblage or who came together to create new assemblages. While creating or joining these assemblages on Twitter, actors employed several processes such as a) retweeting or replying; b) creating hashtags and using them to express stories, opinions, data, and solidarity; and c) creating direct message chat groups. Similarly, on Facebook, actors a) liked, commented, or shared posts; b) created groups or pages that people could join or like; and c) created message groups. These groups helped in forming coalitions via transnational assemblage by bringing people from different countries, time zones, and disciplines together to respond to the earthquake's damage by going against the dominant narratives and practices of disaster response. These practices were mostly led by the volunteers who launched their disaster response efforts by mainly using social media and by forming coalitions. For example, a conversation on Twitter calls out the World Food Programme for distributing rotten rice (see Figure 2.5).

The actor in this case noticed a problem, recorded it, and chose to post it on Twitter in the hopes of bringing widespread attention to the issue so that it could be quickly and appropriately addressed as people's lives depended on it. Had this actor not had access to Twitter as a tool to conduct his activism, the rotten rice problem would have most likely remained a local issue that the organization would have worked to suppress because it made them look bad. Because the actor had access to Twitter, however, the issue gained widespread attention thanks to others replying to and retweeting his post until it went viral. The World Food Programme was then forced to be held accountable for its actions, resulting in the organization working to mend their mistake.

Figure 2.5. Conversation with photographic evidence of how rotten rice was being distributed in Nepali rural communities.

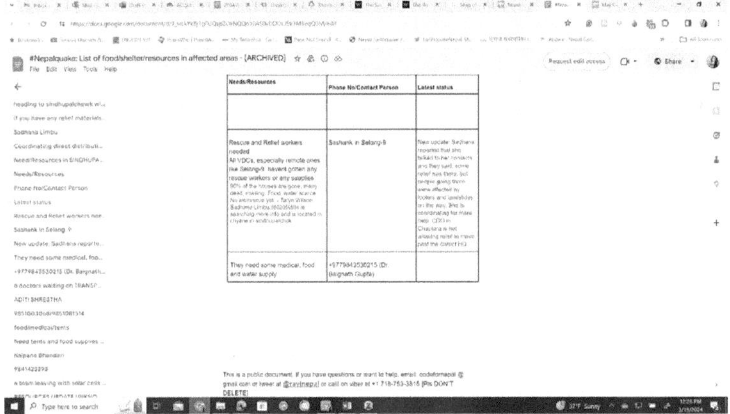


Figure 2.6. Google Doc created by Code for Nepal that acted as a resource for crisis management and communication of needs, resources, and actions in Nepal. The document was managed by Code for Nepal volunteers. (See reference to access the archived document.)

The participants I interviewed shared that they too have used technology to share, seek, validate, and curate information and resources, to organize relief-oriented actions as well as to stand up to the authorities. One of the participants was directly involved with the Nepali government. They were tasked with curating the governmental information website immediately after the disaster. They explained that, after two to three hours of work, they had set up a website to curate official information directly from the government. While they relied on various governmental sources, the participant also used social media platforms to collect and verify the data. After curating this data, the participant would develop governmental responses to support earthquake survivors in need. Similarly, with the help of government data, Code for Nepal, a nonprofit established by a diaspora of young Nepalis in the United States, was curating information in the form of an interactive map. Code for Nepal was also working on a common Google Doc that crowdsourced information about volunteers, relief supplies, emergency services, and communities in need (see Figure 2.6) . Such crowdsourced data helped numerous relief organizations and volunteers to accurately locate specific requests for help and to gather accurate data on what was happening in real time. These insights accentuate the idea that, while the government is a good source of information, it is not a good source for comprehensive information. In other words, social media platforms provided my participant and Code for Nepal with a way to fill the gaps, crowdsource, and gain a holistic idea of how much damage was done and which communities needed support the most because members of these communities were using social media to tell their stories. Because the government is limited by formalities and protocols, it is not possible for all issues to be addressed. That's when other technological tools developed by unofficial disaster responders came into play.

In her article titled "3 Ways Nepalis Are Using Crowdsourcing to Aid in Quake Relief," Shreeya Sinha, a reporter for *The New York Times,* shares the following:

> In the wake of the 7.8 magnitude earthquake that hit their country over the weekend, many Nepalis at home and abroad have found a new way to help—as digital volunteers, spending hours hunched over their laptops, using crowdsourcing technologies and social platforms to participate in the relief effort. (Sinha, n.p.)

Living up to this assessment, one of my participants noticed a gap in relief supply, so they created a web-based platform to provide supply chain management for relief necessities. Likewise, two Nepali diasporas who had established a non-governmental, volunteer-based organization were using web-based platforms, including Google Docs, Facebook, and Twitter, to organize relief, conduct surveys, and prepare data visualizations. Some of my participants explained that many Nepalis around the world employed Google Docs to coordinate relief-oriented actions. The volunteers achieved this by searching for the communities that the government or other larger organizations had yet to reach. An organization named Kathmandu Living Labs created Humanitarian Open Street Maps (HOT), a service that creates maps of high-vulnerability areas where data is scarce ("Disaster Activation"). Facebook and Google responded to the Nepal earthquake by activating new features during the earthquake. Google activated a technology called People Finder that helped relatives and friends locate their loved ones, and Facebook launched its Safety Check feature to determine whether people in the disaster-affected area were safe. One Nepali participant was contacted by Facebook before the Safety Check was launched:

> Google . . . created its Crisis Mark [and] Facebook [has its] Safety Check. [Before Facebook had set up its Safety Check], I talked

> to one of the [Facebook] VPs . . . and asked if we could set up the Safety Checks through Facebook. I do not think [the Safety Check] work[ed] much. They [Facebook] got to know about the disaster in Nepal, and I think they did care about that. (Participant from Nepal)

While larger global platforms were creating support systems after the earthquake, people created their own innovative solutions that allowed them to properly curate, manage, and validate information, which aided them in organizing disaster response in an equitable manner, something that the government alone would not have been able to achieve. This is another example of *swa-byabasthapan*, where people were using technologies creatively to manage the large-scale disaster on their own.

Nepalis at home and abroad were maximizing the use of social media and responding to the disaster by going against the traditional practice of waiting for the government or other organizations to come and support the affected communities and by forming or being part of transnational assemblages. Many of my participants said that they used social media platforms to share pictures and information, disprove fake news, and curate reports on their blogs. Various researchers conducting studies on the role of Twitter during disasters (Cho et al.; Crooks et al.; Potts) have argued that the role of social media during a disaster should be acknowledged because it delivers information to people in a quick and highly efficient way. As with other big disasters, before the public fully recognized the serious damage caused by the earthquake, social media users were already posting their experiences of what was going on in their locality in the digital space (Cho et al.). Curating those personal experiences and sharing them online transformed that knowledge into data that could be used by volunteers to better understand the current state of affairs. This led the Nepali government and other entities to rely on social media platforms so that they could assess the situation and accurately deploy the necessary relief supplies to the affected communities. Transnational assemblages were therefore able to inform the government, media, and other organizations conducting disaster relief about people's needs, and they also helped gather data in a much quicker manner than traditional means. Hence, the transnational assemblages informed by the non-Western disaster response provided a platform for activists to voice suppressed opinions, for the Nepali diaspora to develop life-saving technologies, and for unofficial actors to fill official relief effort gaps.

## ENACTING CRISIS COMMUNICATIONS WITH SOCIAL JUSTICE DURING DISASTER

During the crisis created by the Nepal earthquake, communications were mediated by both official organizations and self-organized transnational assemblages on the internet. The formation of transnational assemblages in the digital web facilitated communications by building as Manuel Castells in *The Rise of Network Society* suggests "a series of locality-based activities and organizations around a key function in the network" (443). Transnational assemblages during the Nepal earthquake facilitated crisis communication that embedded social justice actions. Pamela Walaski defines crisis communications as "those messages that are given to audiences during an emergency event that threatens them either immediately or at some foreseeable point in the near future" (9). Transnational assemblages were collecting and sharing the information and sharing these to larger audiences. These kinds of urgent messages help audiences stay informed, become aware of the situation surrounding the disaster, and create precautionary measures. In informing the public, the role of transnational assemblages became greater than that of dominant practices as they challenged the governmental messages, demanded transparency in information, and enacted their own forms of communication.

In conducting such crisis communications, participants organized data collection by mobilizing volunteers on the ground, by translating data, and by curating information on websites in multimodal forms while also putting the major agenda of communicating for social justice at the heart of their efforts. In *Rhetoric of a Global Epidemic*, Huiling Ding argues that technical communicators have a civic responsibility in these kinds of crises to ensure that communication carried out through the necessary outlets is conveyed effectively so that the largest amount of people can benefit from such communication. My participants agreed with this notion and revealed that they shared information via Twitter, curated reports on blogs or in Facebook groups, organized relief, and constructed various data visualizations to provide relief statistics on Google Docs. My participants carefully chose which platform to use depending on the information that they posted, the format this information would take, and the audience they wanted the information to reach. Formal organizations were not so nimble in crisis communications. As noted earlier in this chapter, the international networks of various humanitarian organizations such as the United Nations, the European Union, and the Red Cross that have a historical presence in Nepal assisted the Nepali government in disaster response and crisis communication. These organizations coordinated with the government, media, and other community-based organizations in Nepal to gather information and share it via their websites and their social media accounts. However, the United Nations, which was a leader of the disaster response effort in Nepal, was criticized for its "situational reports" because their accounts targeted donors and not the community. While the situation reports were one of the communication mechanisms and were very important, one participant shared that they did not represent community voices. The participant stated:

> There was always a daily number of coordination meetings, and I [joined them]. At this point, there's nobody there except the UN and a couple of big organizations. So, I felt that, okay, there was a lot of space for me to inject the communication components. The UN would be thinking, and [all they were worried about were these] situation reports [and they would wonder] how to bring [communication components and the report] together. But I was like, okay, I'm not talking about . . . a situation report. I am talking about talking to the community. So how are we going to do that quickly, and how can we ensure that it's a . . . meaningful process? (Participant from Nepal who is non-Nepali and based in Nepal)

The participant later mentioned that, in an effort to give the local community a voice, she mobilized her team to reach out to the public and gather data and stories from the local people. After gathering the information, that same participant's organization aired a show, which had 6.6 million subscribers and viewers, on Facebook, where she told the people's stories and relayed important information that would keep everyone safe. Hence, the participant's organization was the first to conduct a need-based survey of that population online and distribute that data to other organizations like the UN to aid in disaster response efforts. Later, the participant's organization also created a very short narrative-based radio program that discussed disaster response efforts. This program was created under the communications protocol adopted by the participant's organization, which allowed community members to tell their stories and provide information on how to respond to disaster-related issues like the water crisis and problems related to open defecation after the earthquake. This community-based program became immensely popular in Nepal after the earthquake as the community could share their knowledge of how to respond to the earthquake. Disaster responders who were in organizational capacities, like my participant, needed to be innovative because the users to whom they were providing information were not only passive listeners, they were also active responders. These organizations also depended on the retweets, responses, shares, and likes of users to whom they were communicating the information.

And as articulated by the participants, even though the government was trying to disseminate information, their efforts were not enough because people needed quick answers and aid to save their lives. Hence, to avoid rumors, to organize relief and rescue efforts, and to reach out to the communities that were ignored by larger organizations, the participants conducted their own crisis communications. Participants shared that since the Nepali government had limited human resources and communication mechanisms to handle the catastrophic disaster, it was slower than local efforts and required a lot of volunteers to enhance such communication. Therefore, Nepali activists relied on social media and the grapevine informational network to access information from the community. One participant shared:

> I was answering these questions for one hour, staying up, and feeling like a crazy thing. I was trying to figure out information, trying to share information, trying to locate people and help people feel better, and in some cases trying to share the unfortunate news. (Participant from Nepal who was based in the US)

During the time of the earthquake, the participant created his own relief work and was not affiliated with any organization. He served as a communication point for many other people in his network. Even though there were official mechanisms for people finding, people outside of Nepal needed the information about their loved ones immediately. The participant shared that Nepal is a close-knit society, and information travels from family, friends, and friends of friends, so it was easier to locate information about people from the people without waiting for official mechanisms to intervene. Another participant mentioned that she was involved in translating governmental information from Nepali to English to make information accessible to non-Nepali speakers who were trying to locate information about their loved ones. Yet another participant collected various reports from sites that were sharing misinformation and addressed those falsities in his blog so that people could get accurate information. Activists in Nepal and beyond conducted crisis communication by mobilizing their resources to get accurate and valid information about the ignored and marginalized communities within the country and shared those via transnational assemblages. A Google Doc from Code for Nepal represents this multiplicity and transnational assemblages very nicely. Communication, coordination, and disaster relief management occur simultaneously in this document where the information is consolidated in one space where people from the US, Nepal, and other countries could work together. The organizer of this Google Doc (see Figure 2.6), Ravi Nepal, and some of his colleagues were in the United States while composing this document. Transnational assemblage actors also curated such information on social media to conduct relief and rescue activities and to hold the government and other disaster-responding organizations accountable. This way of communicating, coordinating, and organizing disaster response is also another example of *swa-byabasthapan*, and in this example's context, it is showcased in communication during the earthquake to manage the consequences of the earthquake.

The Google document (see Figure 2.6) is an example of transnational assemblages formed during the Nepal earthquake that provided a public voice for communities who were being ignored. Such communications within the transnational assemblages were flexible, adaptive, and did not have any official protocols; as you can see in the photo, there is a Viber number shared (see Figure 2.6). While repurposing such messages with social media functions like sharing, retweeting, liking, or replying, and sometimes rewriting, the crisis communication practices in the wake of the Nepal earthquake blurred the boundaries between the official and unofficial networks. Crisis communications are mostly employed in an organizational context (Walaski); however, my data suggests that, because the context of the world is continuously transforming during a crisis, crisis communication is also always transforming. In this context, catastrophic disasters invite multiple stakeholders, organizations, and various evolving assemblages to communicate about the crisis and aid in the disaster response effort. To manage a successful disaster response, stronger crisis communication mechanisms that involve and highlight the role of the community and the people who are involved in disaster response are required (Coombs and Holladay; Horsley and Barker; Walaski).

Figure 2.7. Tweet by Aakar Anil in which he shares photos of an immediate gathering of people for relief and open space.

Crisis communication has changed over the past 40 years, and it mostly involves responding to crises that are becoming increasingly global as their causes and consequences transcend national and cultural boundaries (Schwarz et al.). A multitude of actors representing governments, NGOs, private organizations, media houses, and local people perform crisis communications. For example, Figure 2.7 showcases information including photos shared by a Kathmandu local right after the Nepal earthquake. This is an example of how actors within various transnational assemblages who engage in seeking, interpreting, and distributing messages are regarded as crisis publics by various crisis communication scholars (Coombs and Holladay; Frandsen and Johansen; Walaski). These crisis publics engage in disaster communications and are an integral part within the transnational assemblages to respond to a disaster. In doing so, they become a part of various assemblages that are either affected by the crisis or are working to respond to the crisis. In this process, crisis publics establish spaces thanks to the flows created by crisis communication. The actors, or the crisis publics, of the Nepal earthquake are such examples. The disaster brought people from around the globe together, forming the transnational assemblages.

In the case of Nepal, Rajib Subba and Tung Bui found that media engagement not only helped to provide services to marginalized communities, but it also helped hold the Nepal police accountable and transparent. My research demonstrates that during the first weeks after the disaster events, the Nepal earthquake changed the dynamics and the rhetorical nature of crisis communication. The public became not only passive receivers of crisis communication, but they also became active responders, interpreters, and transmitters of information (Coombs and Holladay). These active roles, as my analysis of the actors' narratives suggests, allowed the actors to take on prominent roles, either by initiating their own assemblages or by becoming part of already established assemblages. Even though there were major actors who performed crisis communication immediately following these events, such as the government and media sources, the active crisis publics who posted information on social media platforms became the most critical actors in the crisis communications that emerged. Social media allowed crisis publics to share their affective reactions immediately and join conversations by becoming part of various transnational assemblages via hashtags or using functions like replying or retweeting. The decentralized communications structure in most social media means that these platforms provide different communicative affordances during disasters (Murthy and Gross), such as interpretations of messages, individual expressions, and criticisms of official organizations. During a time of a disaster, digital tools empower people to express themselves and perform crisis communication. Erin Frost, in her analysis of risk communication during the Deepwater Horizon crisis, found that the persuasive messages written by local communicators were often more helpful than the messages from professional communicators at major media outlets. This is because local communicators witness and experience the consequences of a crisis firsthand; thus, their messages are honest, powerful, and meaningful.

## CONCLUSION: NON-WESTERN DISASTER RESPONSE

Transnational assemblages that formed during the Nepal earthquake managed the disaster and conducted crisis communication by developing disaster response practices—practices which contained the values of social justice and critiqued Western crisis management strategies. As such, their unique ways of communicating and managing disaster led to the formation of assemblages that prioritized the community's needs. Some of the common themes of non-Western disaster response included a) contextualizing the information based on the audience of the messages, b) involving the community and their local knowledge of resisting disaster and curating that information on social media, c) reusing the information created by the official channels and simplifying it by visualizing the data and information, d) questioning the authorities to provide accurate information, and e) conducting disaster relief on the ground with social justice. Nepal's non-Western ways of communication had one purpose: to achieve social justice for the marginalized population who was suffering and ignored in the process of disaster relief. The transnational assemblages that operated via non-Western methods defined their boundaries based on social justice, and they maintained those boundaries throughout the disaster response effort. The non-Western disaster response described by the Nepalis could be summarized as follows:

- **Swa-byabasthapan:** The Nepali community demonstrated *swa-byabasthapan*, loosely translated to "self-management" in English. Actors self-managed when they spontaneously launched disaster response efforts that targeted the most needy, marginalized, and vulnerable people and conducted disaster management with social justice. As there was a lot of distrust of the government, the people did not wait for someone else to come and rescue them. Instead, through their self-management, Nepalis were able to form transnational assemblages to organize and perform coalitional actions for disaster management. This action, grounded in the non-Western values of self-reliance and working together with each other, helped mitigate the disaster's challenges with grounding on social justice.

- **Community Values (Being Nepali):** A lot of Nepalis shared that, regardless of location, they were grounded in the community values and beliefs of being Nepali. Nepalis had a sense of responsibility to their community and felt motivated to participate in disaster response efforts without a second thought. In turn, Nepali community values motivated a lot of non-Nepalis to support Nepal in its time of need and non-Nepalis also became part of transnational assemblages in launching disaster response.
- **Resistance and Agency:** Nepalis showcased a strong resistance to the government, international agencies, and media outlets. This agency was a big part of disaster response efforts in Nepal as it allowed the transnational assemblages to decentralize information and expedite aid delivery. While the government and other organizations were doing their best, they were overwhelmed. The transnational assemblages that developed with solidarity at the forefront of their efforts were able to provide actual support to the people who needed the most help. Actors also embodied this resistance when they asked for help from the international community as opposed to their own government.
- **Disaster Activism:** The non-Western disaster response in Nepal was characterized by activism that involved transnational assemblages from across the world focused on social justice for the affected community. This activism showcased how Nepalis could really bring the world together and create space for discussion, empathy, money, and disaster relief. This kind of activism, informed by transparency and social justice, was motivated by affect and organized with assorted technological apparatuses. This allowed the Nepali community to invite the global community to participate in their activism.

In this chapter, I summarized how Nepalis and non-Nepalis responded to the Nepal earthquake in 2015. Nepalis resisted the governmental and international humanitarian organizations' rhetoric while also collaborating with them. The management of crisis as showcased by the transnational assemblages in Nepal demonstrates that crisis management should be understood from a perspective that focuses on the receiver, not the donor, actively representing the various voices of marginalized populations. Communication in any circumstance should not privilege one single voice, and during the aftermath of a calamity, disaster managers should work toward not privileging one voice. Disaster managers should involve the community in responding to the crisis and performing crisis communication because doing so helps make communication effective and relevant. The aftermath of a disaster requires very sensitive and effective communication because a crisis changes the dynamics, needs, and reactions of the community that is suffering. Crisis communications should therefore incorporate the notion of social justice (Walton et al.) that can support the marginalized and vulnerable communities affected by the disaster.

# 3

# Decolonial Approaches of Disaster Response during Hurricane Maria in Puerto Rico

I was with my partner during the hurricane in my home in San Juan, Puerto Rico. We are kind of used to preparing for hurricane season, so, we thought the usual drills we do communication-wise once the hurricane passed would suffice. But as communications went down, we began to worry. Then the power went out completely. To communicate with my family, I wasn't worried. I live close, so I could walk and be with them in a matter of minutes. When the hurricane was ongoing, my family was at their home, and I was at my home. Afterwards, we spent a lot of time together and we helped each other. Regarding the communication with friends, that was trickier because, here in Puerto Rico, cell phone coverage was down. I don't know for how long, but I know that the calls would drop when I tried to reach out. That was really bad. In my case, I had AT&T, and the text sometimes worked. There was no internet or Wi-Fi, none of that, for some time. A year and a half has already passed, so, I don't remember the exact timeframe, but I do remember being cut off from my friends. When the internet signal for the cell phone came back, I found that WhatsApp was a good way to communicate because you could send the message and, even if it didn't go through in that moment, at some point it would. Another good thing about WhatsApp is that you could monitor when the person you are chatting with is online. So that was the way of more or less knowing if the person would receive the message or not. Facebook Messenger was another useful app too.

About 10 days after the hurricane, I started a GoFundMe page to raise money to buy renewable energy items like solar panels and mosquito nets and also to distribute purified water because having

> clean water was an issue as well. Once our communication lines were restored, things got better. I began fundraising, and people from Europe and the United States began donating. I kept receiving donations until May of 2018. At the end of it, I think I raised like $12,000. I was also receiving money outside of the GoFundMe page, and different people shipped items to my home. I also had an Amazon Wishlist. I would share my list with people so that I could let them know what I was buying or what I recommended. People preferred to buy the items themselves, but they would ship them to me. I haven't really done the math, I never counted item by item, but I think that I collected about $15,000 in donations.
>
> – Participant, Puerto Rico

On September 17, 2017, Hurricane Maria struck and devastated many communities throughout Puerto Rico along with several other Caribbean islands. Puerto Rico is an archipelago that was once part of the Spanish Empire and is now a commonwealth of the United States. My participants referred to Puerto Rico as an island during the interviews rather than using the word *archipelago.* Puerto Rico's political status is under constant debate, with some in favor of statehood, others independence, and still others who favor the continuation of commonwealth status. These differing stances create a constant dilemma over sovereignty ("Puerto Rico: History and Heritage"). Puerto Rico is prone to hurricanes, storms, and earthquakes. Every year there is hurricane season that people prepare for as the participant mentioned above. And unlike the Nepal earthquake, which came suddenly, hurricanes and their strength can be predicted by meteorologists and scientists. However, no one had anticipated the devastation and damage that Hurricane Maria would go on to cause. According to a study conducted by Kishore et al. (2018), "Maria caused an estimated $90 billion in damages, making it the third costliest tropical cyclone in the United States since 1900" (163). Additionally, the *Regional Overview: Impacts of Hurricanes Irma and Maria* claimed that 169,000 people and 75,000 buildings were exposed to wind speeds that surpassed 252 km/hr.

The official death count in Puerto Rico was 64; however, Kishore et al. claimed that the death toll exceeded 4,645 people, which is 70 times more than the official estimate. After this report was published, Puerto Ricans rallied with a symbolic demonstration of shoes that belonged to the people in San Juan who were killed by the hurricane. An online hashtag, #4645, was also created to protest the official death count (see Figures 3.1 and 3.2). After the controversy surrounding the death toll, the governor of Puerto Rico commissioned the Milken Institute School of Public Health at George Washington University to conduct an independent study. In this report, the death toll was revised and estimated to be 2,975 people (Milken Institute School of Public Health). The institute found that physicians had a lack of awareness of appropriate death certification practices and that the governor's lack of communication about death certificates had created the death count problem (Milken Institute School of Public Health). Carmen D. Zorrilla in her article "The View from Puerto Rico—Hurricane Maria and its Aftermath" argues that, in contrast to other sudden disasters, hurricanes often allow officials to be prepared. "Yet our infrastructure, including the health care infrastructure was already in crisis" (1801). This was also because Hurricane Irma had hit Puerto Rico just two weeks before Maria.

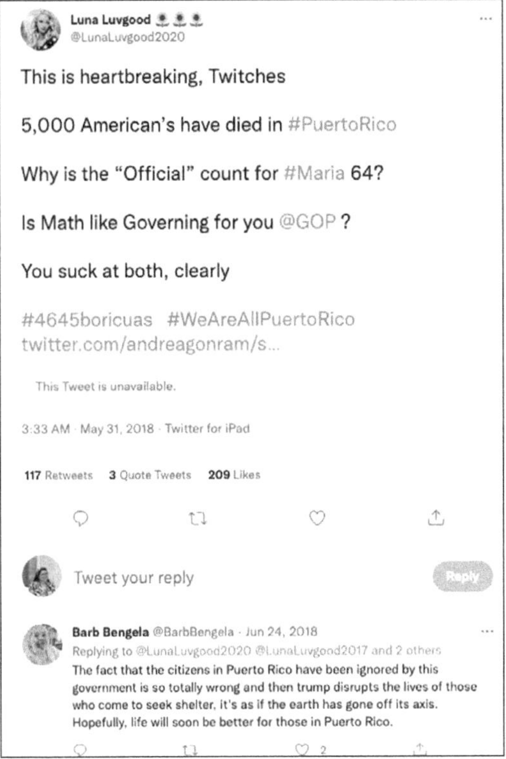


Figure 3.1. Conversation on Twitter that used the Hashtag #4645Boricuas.

Figure 3.2. Tweet showcasing a public protest on June 2, 2018, regarding the death count of Hurricane Maria.

Public life in Puerto Rico came to a standstill due to the unexpected amount of damage, which also caused large-scale power outages and communication disruptions. Hurricane Maria has been regarded as one of the most catastrophic events to devastate cities in Puerto Rico and other Caribbean islands. And much like the Nepal earthquake, Hurricane Maria exacerbated the vulnerability of the communities in Puerto Rico who have suffered through "an ongoing recession, insurmountable debt, and coloniality" (Soto Vega n.p.). Lloréns argues that Hurricane Maria also brought endemic risks, vulnerabilities, and hidden crises into view, affecting people who are infirm, people who are disabled, people without access to transportation, those living in isolated areas, and those in extreme poverty with greater intensity (159). The lack of electric power and mobile phone networks after the hurricane also caused a serious communication crisis which cut the island off from the rest of the world. The hurricane also brought to light the ongoing sovereignty struggles. It highlighted how the severity of colonialist protocols and negligence by the US government impacted the most vulnerable. (In my interviews, all of the Puerto Rican participants articulated discomfort with the colonization of Puerto Rico.) As a consequence, Hurricane Maria caused countless Puerto Ricans to relocate to the US mainland. A report written by Jennifer Hinojosa and Edwin Meléndez and published by the Center for Puerto Rican Studies, *Puerto Rican Exodus: One Year Since Hurricane Maria*, suggests that 159,415 (and up to 176,603) Puerto Ricans have relocated to the United States in the year since Hurricane Maria made landfall in Puerto Rico.

Similar to response efforts after the Nepal earthquake, various organizations (private and public) inside and outside of Puerto Rico were involved in relief and rescue activities, with a significant engagement by the United States. From the social web to the wider Puerto Rican diaspora (particularly the diaspora in the United States), Puerto Ricans formed a variety of networked communities or transnational assemblages to address the aftermath of Hurricane Maria. There is, however, one factor that differentiates Puerto Rico's situation from Nepal's. In Puerto Rico, the use of technology was not as powerful as it was in Nepal. This is because the hurricane disrupted electricity sources, telecommunication, and internet access. Despite this, there were some people and organizations, such as Burger King, that opened to provide meals to people that included internet access ("Burger King's recovery"). A lot of people also relied on unreliable internet connections to send messages on WhatsApp and publish posts on Facebook. Also, unlike with the 2015 Nepal earthquake, Mark Zuckerberg, the CEO of Facebook, did not raise funds for Puerto Rico on his personal Facebook page. Some news stories, however, described a partnership between the Red Cross and Facebook in which the two companies would work together to build "population maps" ("Mark Zuckerberg Tours"). In October 2017, Mark Zuckerberg also shared a livestream video of a virtual reality avatar of himself in Puerto Rico, but this livestream was highly criticized by people who regarded him as "a heartless billionaire" and accused him of "exploiting disaster" ("Mark Zuckerberg Apologizes").

Another aspect that distinguishes the two disasters is the United States' Federal Emergency Management Agency's (FEMA) involvement in the disaster response efforts. In contrast to Nepal, because FEMA was an active responder in Puerto Rico, there were already established technology-based applications like a Twitter account, FEMA's official Facebook page, and a website with information and reporting features that actors could use in case of emergency. Likewise, the Puerto Rico government also had their own disaster response page. Additionally,

United for Puerto Rico was an initiative brought forth by the then First lady of Puerto Rico, Mrs. Beatriz Rosselló, which was criticized by the people. After the declaration of a major disaster in Puerto Rico, FEMA configured this website to share all the available information regarding Hurricane Maria both in English and in Spanish (https://www.fema.gov/disaster/4339/). Even though the technology was virtually useless due to unreliable electricity and telecommunications, many people outside of Puerto Rico managed to use technology for information on support, even if that support did not include FEMA's state-funded outlets. The reason for this seeming avoidance of official channels was primarily due to FEMA's formal requirements that needed to be satisfied for victims to receive state-funded relief. For example, people who had generational family houses were affected by FEMA's requirements since they were not able to receive the relief without presenting proof of home ownership. As Ivis Garcia shares, Puerto Rico has a history of informal construction and an estimate of 260,000 homes in Puerto Rico do not have titles or deeds (21). Furthermore, in "The Housing Crisis in Puerto Rico and the Impact of Hurricane Maria," Jennifer Hinojosa and Edwin Meléndez report that "Of the total of 772, 682 valid homeowners registrations, only 40 percent were approved for FEMA assistance." There was a lack of governmental support in Puerto Rico in the post-hurricane context. These sorts of situations resulted in the creation of transnational assemblages who supported these families who, due to government protocols, would otherwise not be supported.

Much like actors in the wake of the Nepal earthquake, then, many disaster responders and grassroots activists both on the island and the mainland launched a decentralized disaster response effort that, given Puerto Rico's colonized status, was informed by decolonial practices (Lloréns; Ortiz Torres; Soto Vega). As such, my case study of Hurricane Maria will highlight how, much like Nepalis, Puerto Ricans created a transnational assemblage to resist Western practices by not relying on the government. To document their accomplishments, I again present the results of my narrative inquiry, this time involving 14 Puerto Rican activists, community-based organizers, and journalists, to showcase the survival practices of marginalized communities who have navigated the oppressive legacy of colonialist systems to restore peace and stability in their communities. The participants articulated intersectional identities that allowed them to take a nuanced understanding of their communities. For example, one of the community members worked specifically in a community in Loiza with Black Puerto Ricans who live below the poverty line. Considering such community-based factors of disaster response in the analysis of the data has been important for this project. I then supplement this analysis by focusing on over 2,000,000 Tweets that were posted during the first week after Hurricane Maria to show how people in Puerto Rico and around the globe responded to the disaster. With these results, I introduce the decolonial approaches to disaster response and address how Puerto Ricans used various digital technologies to respond to the crisis their communities were facing.

## TRANSNATIONAL ASSEMBLAGES WITH DECOLONIAL DISASTER RESPONSE STRATEGIES

After the devastating hurricane and the lack of support from the US government, Puerto Ricans took charge of disaster relief efforts in their own communities by implementing a decolonial approach to disaster response. Based on my participants' framing of their actions, supplemented by the work of decolonial scholars, I define decolonial disaster response in the context of Hurricane Maria as developing an alternative, grassroots disaster response that resisted colonial power and paradigms of disaster relief practices through recognizing community needs (Quijano). This means that Puerto Ricans, like Nepalis, did not wait for US government or local Puerto Rico government assistance to reach Puerto Rico before taking action. Such government assistance came with a lot of bureaucracy, which slowed or blocked aid from reaching the people who needed it the most and didn't provide support to the ones who needed it due to lack of documentation. For example, homeowners are eligible to receive FEMA assistance only if they have official papers showing home ownership (Talbot et al.). Puerto Ricans had to overcome colonial history and administration which restricts any international countries or their governments from sending food and aid to Puerto Rico. And what made the situation even worse was that aid was not being managed properly by the Puerto Rican government, the only country authorized to send supplies. As a result, much of the aid was parked in trailers and remained in cargo ships while people were suffering.

In response to such inefficiencies, Puerto Ricans created alternative processes for giving and receiving aid by developing cross-diasporic communicative opportunities, a situation which was similar to what Nepalis did in delivering aid and relief to the communities in need.

That is, personally developed transnational assemblages stepped in to help. Such transnational assemblages allowed personal and religious networks to participate in disaster relief actions. Not only that, there were community-based, smaller organizations that could draw upon larger networks for support. For example, churches became a network point for a lot of volunteers, relief providers, and activists. Churches had pre-existing networks and knew their communities better, so they became hubs for assorted relief-related activities (Petrun Sayers et al.). As is well known, Puerto Rico has a large Catholic population, and attending church is a central part of cultural and religious life in Puerto Rico. Hence, during and after Hurricane Maria, churches became spaces where people could not only find information and learn about people's whereabouts, but they also acted as spaces for relief operations that supported other organizations. There are around 1,500 churches in Puerto Rico, and all the major churches that have a website had some information about disaster recovery. Additionally, various interviewees also mentioned churches a lot as either being part of them or working together with them.

Many participants also articulated that one of the reasons why their disaster relief work was successful was due to the transnational connections they forged on social media. Puerto Ricans created the majority of their networks through the Puerto Rican diaspora in the United States, through religious networks primarily mediated by the Catholic Church, and through the networks within their own locales. With the help of these networks, the participants were able to raise funds, carry out relief activities, and support communities in need. The participants echoed these strategies by highlighting that they reached out to their interpersonal networks and beyond to seek help, build communities, and support communities that had already established networks or were newly formed. Four participants represented community-based organizations that participated in community-based activities. One of them represented a food bank in Puerto Rico that included networks of more than 100 smaller organizations that helped in the distribution of food after Hurricane Maria. One participant represented a feminist organization that relied on its community leaders' networks to distribute disaster relief. Six participants mentioned the use of social media platforms like Facebook or GoFundMe to raise money throughout their networks. Three participants represented private organizations in Puerto Rico. These private organizations had connections in the

United States and beyond that allowed the participants to support the suffering communities. Three participants who represented the media mentioned that the networks of journalists on the island and beyond the United States made it easier to share information within both the community and a larger network. The religious network was also mentioned by five participants, who described how the church became a space for people to come together and organize relief efforts.

The havoc created by Hurricane Maria not only devastated land and communities, but it also revealed issues in aid distribution and colonialism, which further exacerbated the lack of disaster response. While the US government's response to Hurricanes Harvey and Irma, which struck the US mainland around the same time, was very quick and well-funded, the US government seemed indifferent when responding to Hurricane Maria in Puerto Rico. Indeed, they created unprecedented bureaucratic barriers that severely hampered the immediate delivery of disaster relief materials. Here, the Western/colonial disaster response was more focused on their own spaces or "states." They completely ignored Puerto Rico as their territory, never making it a priority of discussion. A study conducted by Charley Willison et al. suggests that "within the first 9 days after the hurricanes hit, both Harvey and Irma survivors had already each received nearly US$100 million in FEMA dollars awarded to individuals and families, whereas Maria survivors had only received slightly over US$6 million in recovery aid" (2). To make matters worse, while the US government was neglecting Puerto Ricans, the Puerto Rican politicians were themselves hoarding supplies and not distributing them. Hence, the decolonial disaster response mediated via transnational assemblages was necessary to make sure that thousands of communities who were suffering would receive what they needed and that the disaster response was equitable and just. As one participant recounted, "There were ships with relief materials in the dock and no one was providing it to the community." This political crisis created the need for transnational assemblages that would position themselves against colonialist practices and actually help the people who needed it.

While people distrusted the governmental relief, Puerto Ricans trusted relief efforts carried out by activists, disaster responders, and volunteers who were in their own individual networks. Such networks created transnational assemblages that included people in the US mainland and beyond. Naomi Klein argues that "deep community relationships, as well as strong ties to the Puerto Rican diaspora, successfully delivered lifesaving aid when the government failed and failed again" (10). The Puerto Rican community collaborated with the diaspora and launched various smaller scale relief efforts that went against protocol and saved people's lives. Dr. Mónica Feliú-Mójer, a Puerto Rican scientist working in the United States, wrote in a blog post that "I started convening with fellow Puerto Ricans living in the United States: How could we help? How could we leverage what we had at our disposal, our networks and resources? I started rallying the community. I became politically active." Just like Dr. Feliú-Mójer, there were many Puerto Ricans who dedicated their time, resources, and networks to disaster response efforts, thus creating their own transnational assemblages.

As in the previous case discussed, transnational assemblages were established by spontaneous actions that motivate people to act during a disaster. Like Dr. Feliú-Mójer, the participants I interviewed understood their actions as being grounded in their commitment toward the community and toward the people who were suffering in parts of Puerto Rico where the mainstream governmental response did not reach. These spontaneous, immediate, or affective actions, along with a sense of commitment, led Puerto Ricans inside and beyond Puerto Rico to create their own volunteer and relief networks, to join transnational assemblages, or work in the online or digital space by forging relationships among numerous other online participants. A participant shared:

> Well, you're not going to believe this, but at the beginning, the first tarps arrived from Australia. I have a Serbian friend who lives in Australia, and she was the first person to react and send tarps. So, we received tarps from everywhere, from the United States, and Mexico, from Spain, from the nearby islands. Afterwards, well, we created a website with a donate button, and we just made all our documents for the IRS and for the government of Puerto Rico to become an NGO. People have seen our work via our Facebook page, so they realize that we're a serious group and that their money is arriving where [it] is needed, so people kept donating. The last donation was a cargo van that we really needed because we were using [volunteers'] cars to transport everything, materials, tools, everything. People donate tools,

> people donate building materials, and it's been a wonderful journey. (Participant from Puerto Rico)

This narrative showcases an example of a transnational assemblage that formed thanks to donations from networks outside of Puerto Rico, where the participant received tarps from Australia. However, to continue this work, the participant formalized that assemblage by registering it as a nonprofit organization so that they could continue to support the community. Thus, as a result of formal US aid distribution and support not reaching the community, community members established and formalized their own network so they could continue to do the work that the government failed to do. This narrative further demonstrates how Facebook was used as a platform for donations and for showcasing accountability. It also highlights how people in Puerto Rico were not networking exclusively among each other within the vicinity of their own country or region. Instead, Puerto Ricans were creating connections beyond their borders. In doing so, they formed transnational assemblages by using personal connections. Puerto Ricans encouraged donations, and for one participant their transnational assemblage helped in creating a formal organization. People depended on their respective diaspora, and people who identified as members of the diaspora also became involved via social media. Thanks to my participants' recollections, it has become clear that, when responding to compounding crisis, actors exercised rhetorical agency in the form of activism and responsibility to the community by establishing transnational assemblages. The participants stated that the massive destruction created by the hurricane made them feel responsible toward the communities that were suffering throughout the island, which is very similar to the Nepali community. Social media platforms became excellent tools used to invite donations from people within and outside of Puerto Rico and the United States. Therefore, such transnational assemblages were driven by anger, empathy, and emotions that made them feel affective responsibility toward their community.

To further address Puerto Ricans' tendency to formalize their assemblages due to government shortcomings, participants recognized a need for coalitional action premised on their own community traditions that were against the formal government officials' normative standard—*autogestión,* loosely translated as *self-management.*

The participants and other actors were able to establish transnational assemblages by prioritizing the voices and needs of the people and by creating flexible protocols that continued to evolve as the crisis unfolded. Soto Vega cites this "autogestión," where Puerto Ricans and people in the diaspora responded to the needs of their fellow countrymen through a coalitional counter-praxis of survival (40–41). Such counter-praxis meant that people were not waiting for governments in Puerto Rico or the United States to follow their protocols; instead, actors were actively responding to the needs of the people by forming connections and by using digital media platforms. Walton et al. state that "fundamentally, it is multiple marginalized groups that have demonstrated the need for coalitional action, and their voices and priorities should centrally inform those actions" (134). For example, the Puerto Rico Somos Gente group, which began as an informal group that formed as a result of a Facebook callout requesting people to join the relief efforts after the hurricane, is now established as an NGO. Today, Puerto Rico Somos Gente continues to reconstruct and rebuild communities that were devastated by Hurricane Maria. The registration of Puerto Rico Somos Gente as an organization makes it a formal transnational assemblage as it moved out from Facebook and informal disaster response work to a formalized response. The formation of multiple networks like Puerto Rico Somos Gente demonstrates that there was a need for aid after the calamity that the government and other official channels were simply unable to provide; thus, it fell on the people to work together to formalize an organization to respond to the disaster according to the suffering community's needs.

Sometimes, it was not necessary for such transnational assemblages to formalize. This is because there were already other international organizations that engaged with community-based organizations in Puerto Rico to help and support the communities, such as Doctors Without Borders or the Catholic Church. Like the diaspora, my participants' international connections were very important in creating transnational assemblages for post-hurricane relief and reconstruction. A participant recounted:

> About two or three months after the hurricane, we did see a couple of different international groups that would come in to help. We assigned them to different jobs. So, for example, we rescued a park that was completely destroyed by the hurricane.

> The kids obviously don't have any way to sort of clear their mind of this disaster that's going around, so we decided to restore that park. And we also received construction materials, and so those international volunteers were also there helping us unload the trucks. But we also had volunteers, and we still have volunteers that go directly to different houses to help reconstruct houses. (Participant from Puerto Rico)

Likewise, a participant from Puerto Rico representing an international private organization explained how his company collaborated with his church to provide relief. In Puerto Rico, various churches are tied to the community, which means that they know who needs the most help and what is happening with which family. This type of community knowledge was very helpful in supporting people in need during the hurricane. The participant recounts:

> At that moment, we put all our merchandise in a church that the city told us to take it to, a [specific] church because they were taking care of . . . giving it away to everybody. It was an excellent opportunity to serve all the people because even though we as employees had hard times, the company was making it easier for us. (Participant from Puerto Rico)

As the participant noted, the company wanted to serve the people in need and provided relief materials to the church that helped them support the community. Other participants have also articulated that they were working with the church or using that space for relief distribution. Some mentioned that people representing the church networks from Latin America came to Puerto Rico to support the communities. This is an excellent example of how religious networks with other countries came to support Puerto Rico in its time of need. Thus, community members who had transnational connections either via their job or via their personal or religious networks were able to connect to these networks and help in the formation of transnational assemblages that supported the community in Puerto Rico.

In responding to compounding crises, Puerto Ricans necessarily developed compounding solutions. In addition to formalizing assemblages and using their connections to official organizations outside of the country, Puerto Ricans also created their own disaster relief mobile application which became a space where people could come together to volunteer and gather data. Connect Relief, a mobile-based application, was created in the aftermath of Hurricane Maria because Puerto Ricans could not rely on the larger technology giants, whose services were spotty while communication lines were down. The application invited hundreds of people to join a transnational assemblage that helped in deconstructing aid distribution by involving people in the community, volunteers, and donors. This application helped collect data, identify community needs, and match donors and volunteers with needy communities. A participant who was part of development of the app and used Connect Relief and trained others in using it shared the following:

> We develop these apps where we collect the information. When the person that is collecting the information through the app is in an area that has internet, like Burger King . . . it goes into our cloud and then it gets categorized in a database, and then we can make it public through maps, through Excel tables. We recruited them through friends of friends of friends, through the diaspora. A lot of people came to Puerto Rico to help. Most of them were college students. The universities in Puerto Rico were closed. Everybody had an urge to go out and help. They were helping us collect data and helping in any way that we needed. It was a monumental effort. It was like me, and like four volunteers, and then 600 volunteers in the streets. We would train groups of 10 to 20, 50, 100 people. We did a couple of trainings via Facebook Live. We would train pastors in churches, and then they would train their congregation. We trained nurses, and they trained other nurses. We trained, you name it, social workers. We've trained psychologists. Nobody had work, so everybody was wanting to go out and help. (Participant from Puerto Rico)

The use of mobile applications like Connect Relief disrupted the traditional way of disaster response and decolonized aid distribution, volunteer management, and disaster relief. The Connect Relief application created an alternate channel of communication and gathering people to conduct disaster response as opposed to the formal disaster response being organized by the government. The app was able to help many volunteers, relief providers, and survivors of Hurricane Maria as data and information are always crucial during a disaster.

Since the application was grassroots-based, it was made available to diverse actors who could help just by uploading the data that they could find in the community. This application and the network of people who used it helped volunteers understand the extent of the damage caused by the hurricane and also provided a better picture of what the needs of the community were. It provided aid where aid wasn't reaching and provided information for volunteers to access the community, which is an example of how the app was able to decolonize the aid distribution and disaster management. This relief effort was managed through a network of networks, including the diaspora who went to serve the communities and not to gain any benefits from them. Through this application, there were fewer protocols that hindered official aid distribution. The transnational assemblages this application created allowed many volunteers from within the community, diaspora, and other parts of the world that were previously unable to help due to government restrictions to participate in the relief effort.

As I discussed above, the decolonial disaster response showcases challenging of the colonial terms and conditions in Puerto Rico that hinder the community's access to disaster relief materials. The decolonial disaster response was grounded in autogestión, whereas with the Nepalis, it was *swa-byapasthapan*. Puerto Rican disaster responders created networks and coalitions with diaspora and within themselves to challenge the disparities in disaster response. They relied on themselves and transnational assemblages to launch their disaster response in an equitable and socially just manner. In both cases, however, the transnational assemblages were linked to community traditions grounded in their own practices that helped to develop resistant practices to highlight injustices perpetuated by Western-based relief efforts.

## VISUALIZING TRANSNATIONAL ASSEMBLAGES DURING HURRICANE MARIA

The transnational assemblages that emerged during Hurricane Maria were extraordinary because they formed even though there was a lack of reliable electricity or telecommunication services. Puerto Ricans were versatile enough to work around such obstacles and still connect with people not just in the United States but also across the globe, particularly in Latin American countries. As discussed above, Puerto

Ricans created their transnational assemblages due to the inaction of the US government, Puerto Rico government, and their own political leaders. To visualize these transnational assemblages, I conducted a social network analysis (SNA) of tweets that were posted in response to Hurricane Maria.

To conduct this analysis, I collected a total of 20 million tweets that reacted to Hurricane Maria. To narrow the scope of my analysis, tweets or users who were not geotagged were removed from the sample. Hence, I used 2,089,701 tweets for my analysis. In the sample, there was a total of 889,670 users. With my analysis, I examined how transnational assemblages were structured. I explored the dynamics and the relationships within each node to understand how such relations affect the outcome, which, in this context, is disaster response. In analyzing these networks via each node, I conducted a similar examination of networks within various countries and Puerto Rico and what those relationship formations entailed. Figure 3.3 visualizes the users in various countries who engaged with tweets by replying to or retweeting the original post. Countries and continents from where the tweets were sent act as nodes. The larger nodes represent Asia (red), Africa (green), South America (light blue), Oceania (yellow), North America (purple), and Europe (dark blue), and the smaller nodes represent the countries within these continents. These nodes are connected by lines that represent the replies and retweets that were sent among the users. The thickness of the lines represents the strength of the relationships among the nodes. The thicker the lines, the more interactions occurred among users residing in these countries.

The SNA of the Twitter data reveals that the Nepal earthquake received more worldwide attention than Hurricane Maria. The strongest network existed between users from Europe and the United States. There was also a network between users from the US and South America. There is a weaker network between users from Asia and the US. Even though people around the world tweeted, retweeted, or replied, it seems the relationships among various continents and Puerto Rico were weaker than the relationships Nepal had forged in the wake of the earthquake. As might be expected, the United States seems to be the major actor and the most prominent node, which resulted in the United States becoming Puerto Rico's primary connection to the outer world.

Figure 3.3. SNA of the Twitter users residing in various countries in the world during and immediately after Hurricane Maria.

The reason for these weak networked actions seen among replies and retweets could be due to the rest of the world having less knowledge about Puerto Rico or a lack of concern for the country as Puerto Rico is a US territory. Nevertheless, the US seemed to be the prominent actor during Hurricane Maria, and the Puerto Rican population in the US could be the reason for the US being visualized as the major actor. Another reason why Puerto Rico lacked relationships with other continents may also be due to the lack of electricity that resulted from the hurricane. Regardless, as the figure reveals, there were still interactions from around the globe during Hurricane Maria, with all continents having used the hashtag #HurricaneMaria or mentioning Hurricane Maria and Puerto Rico to some degree.

The establishment of transnational assemblages on Twitter was not as prominent as it had been after the Nepal earthquake. Again, this goes back to the argument of how difficult it was for the transnational communities to send aid or even to interact with the communities in Puerto Rico. I would argue that this data showcases how colonial control in the form of policies and protocols did not allow for outside interactions and engagements and the engagements were mostly within the United States and Puerto Rico. Despite such control, however, Puerto Ricans still managed to establish many relationships throughout the globe, relationships that were weaker than Nepal's, but relationships nonetheless. Thus, even though Puerto Rico received less global attention than Nepal, and despite the colonial control, transnational assemblages still materialized and responded to the catastrophe left by Hurricane Maria.

## AGAINST COLONIAL ATTITUDE: TRANSNATIONAL ASSEMBLAGES IN ACTION

The disaster response efforts that took place because of Hurricane Maria would not have been possible without the transnational assemblages functioning as social coalitions formed beyond Puerto Rican boundaries. These coalitions resisted norms and continued to advocate for justice for Puerto Ricans. Such transnational assemblages functioned to take action against the colonial practices in disaster response and to aid delivery. As such, transnational assemblages created affective energy among the people that went beyond emotions and feelings, allowing people to respond to the politics of colonialism. Their decolonial actions were represented in the digital media, and such representations allowed the transnational assemblages to expand and go beyond boundaries and work toward social justice for the communities in Puerto Rico.

Indeed, as has been shown throughout this project, technology use (especially social media platforms) in disaster response situations and other political crises is prominent. During a disaster, people rely on available technologies to seek, share, and validate information (Potts). Just as in Nepal, Puerto Ricans used social media to form social coalitions that allowed them to amplify their voices by engaging with assorted multimodal content and organizing disaster relief efforts. Internet-based fundraising platforms like GoFundMe, collaborative platforms like Google Docs, and other social media spaces like WhatsApp and Amazon Wishlist constituted some of the platforms used in the hurricane's aftermath. Similar to Nepal, social media platforms not only became a space for people to express empathy toward suffering individuals, but they also acted as a place where people could create coalitions across the world and help in organizing disaster relief efforts.

Furthermore, the crisis publics, a major part of transnational assemblages, play the role of an active audience who can talk back to the dominant narratives shared by the government and highlight any discrepancies that emerge during a disaster while also sharing their voices via social media platforms. This act of raising awareness via social media platforms displays the autonomous characteristics of an assemblage (Delanda). Social media platforms create the possibility for understanding the public reaction to a disaster in real time, including the possibility to recognize an emergent crisis public for disaster management (Murthy and Gross; Subba). My participants communicated and performed various kinds of communication practices, such as gathering data and information, taking pictures and posting them, curating videos and sharing them, or creating webpages for donations. These kinds of practices not only helped in responding to the disaster, but they also helped in creating a transnational assemblage where a socially just, decolonial discourse about the disaster could take place. Hence, the crisis communications performed within transnational assemblages created various flows, helping to create the transnational assemblages.

Social media was also a space for people to stand up to colonialism. For example, the tweet shown in Figure 3.4 highlights Puerto Rico's colonial history and brings attention to how 70 percent of the island was still without power 100 days after Hurricane Maria had struck. The colonial rules and regulations upheld by the United States made it very difficult for the Puerto Ricans to receive and distribute aid and also address the issues such as electricity, which is a basic necessity of the people. Hence, it was organizations that have networks all across the island, such as Food Bank, that stepped in to distribute food throughout the island when official means failed.

My participant who represented Food Bank shared their frustration with colonial rules that made it very difficult for people on the island to get disaster-related aid:

> The biggest firm was FEMA. FEMA took over the ports and suddenly, they decided that everything that was coming in, you know, they were going to establish priorities. We had trailers in the ports, sitting there for days waiting for someone to release them to the distribution field. At the beginning, it was disastrous, and it was basically because FEMA took over, it was

very difficult. And then the governor took over and the governor started making distribution, but the distribution was full of trailers for the bank and a couple trailers for people. The politics got involved in the whole process, so their people were getting several trailers, but they didn't have the capacity. They started storing these trailers on farms all over the place, and there they stood for almost a year. You know, until a reporter found out there were trailers all over the place and a lot of food was wasted because it expired. I don't know if there's still thousands of packs of water in Ceiba. (Participant from Puerto Rico)

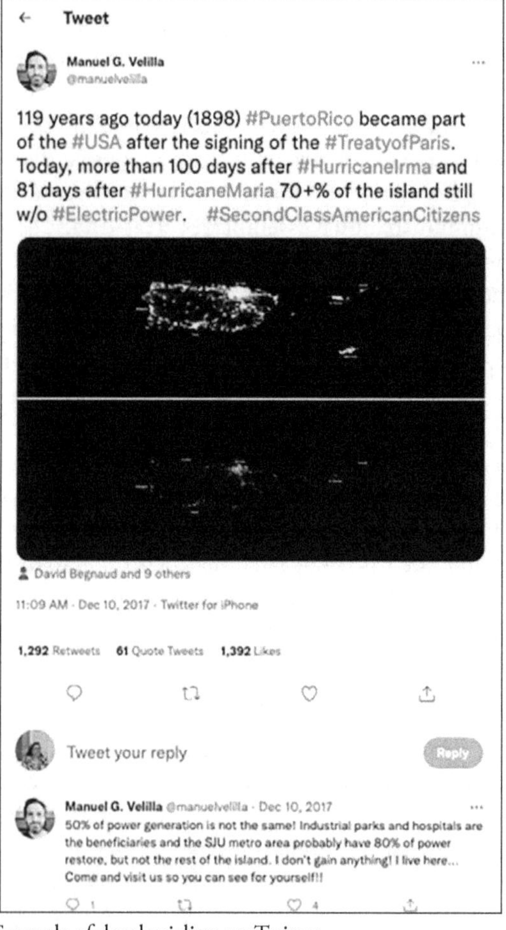


Figure 3.4. Example of decolonialism on Twitter.

While dealing with the reality of undistributed food and aid, the participant's organization, which already had a network of 125 other organizations in Puerto Rico, started distributing food to the people throughout the island. Importantly, Blanca Ortiz Torres argues that "autonomous organizing does not imply removing the state's responsibility to guarantee the basic rights of all citizens. In fact, it implies the opposite, to promote the empowerment/strengthening of citizens and communities to demand what they deserve, when they need it" (363). While there were official disaster response efforts that were not able to reach out to the communities who were the most vulnerable, Puerto Ricans who were capable of supporting their communities were empowering each other, supporting each other by going against the colonial power.

In another narrative, my participant shares their experience of establishing an organization after Hurricane Maria as a spontaneous reaction to the lack of aid and support that the government was able to provide to the communities. They showcase how such coalitions were formed in a moment of chaos:

> Well, the organization began three weeks after the . . . hurricane. Actually, we never thought about making an organization. We thought about helping our neighbors, immediate neighbors at the moment because we noticed that three weeks later, they were living in very difficult conditions. We saw this elder couple every morning pulling out their mattresses, wringing their clothes because they had no roof. So, in the middle of, let's say, in the middle of a feeling of empathy and frustration I wrote in my social media that if I had tarps I would install those [on] my own. People out of the island began reacting like, "I can send you tarps. Where do I send the tarps?" And a couple of weeks later, I had hundreds of tarps in my home. So, I spoke to my neighbors, and we began, we got organized. I have a neighbor that is a social worker, so he prepared these needs assessment forms and we asked for volunteers via Facebook, and people arrived, and we began well, searching, searching for houses without a roof. And this is how everything began. (Participant from Puerto Rico)

My participant noticed how government aid had yet to arrive in their neighborhood. Instead of waiting, as they had already waited for three weeks, they took matters into their own hands and began gathering materials to help their neighbors. This gathering, like for many other organizations that were formed and formalized during Hurricane Maria, began with a social media post.

Indeed, a lot of the participants showcase rhetorical agency against the unreliable government and colonial rules. Going against colonial practices, Puerto Rican communities were motivated to serve and help themselves, which led to the creation of spaces and coalitions in which new "articulations were being forged," thus "constituting a new assemblage or territory" (Slack and Wise 158). Some newer forms of articulations were seen in hashtags, such as #PuertoRicowillRise, or common expressions shared by Puerto Rican participants, such as "something for my people." Another participant shared:

> We told everybody, "Okay, let's go back to our homes, let's sleep through the night, cool it down. Seven AM tomorrow, let's go out with whatever machine, power machine, tools you've got or anything, machetes, whatever you have, we're going to start cleaning the road." Because we couldn't wait for the government. It was so devastating that if we would have waited for the government party, we wouldn't be leaving our homes. (Participant from Puerto Rico)

Likewise, another participant recounted:

> After we formed officially, we started then being able to get volunteers from churches, from friends, and other types of volunteers, and we were able to bring aid and help to 21 towns in Puerto Rico. So, we impacted about 8,000 families, bringing them food, supplies, solar cells, solar lamps, also the tarps for the roofs.
>
> So, we did a GoFundMe, but we've done it now. We didn't do it at that time. So, all this was money that was being given to us by people who were donating for getting all these supplies. And then we also had to rent all the transportations, so all the vans and whatnot, to go to all these places. (Participant from Puerto Rico)

These two narratives are examples of how the participants and their community did not intend to wait for the government to come to their rescue because they knew that they were mostly invisible to both the local and the US government, thus not a priority. These two are some of the many examples of people coming together due to an affective response of "we need to do something," which in turn is responding to the politics that left many marginalized people neglected.

The disaster responder community perceived that the need for relief was immediate. They were motivated to act against the inaction of the governments, a sentiment that was shared by the Nepali people in the wake of the Nepal earthquake. As discussed previously, the desire to act right in the moment is affective, which represents actors' agency that led toward the formation of a transnational assemblage within that specific community for tasks such as cleaning the road or helping people get medicine. Affect helps human beings act, react, or not act in certain situations. Brian Massumi characterizes affect by recognizing the importance of intensity. Events, incidents, and disasters create spontaneous moments where situations are intense and draw global attention, and this intensity makes people act. In transnational assemblages, affect helps bodies form new ties or relationships across the globe or enact new habits and rituals via intercultural understanding and communications, disrupting the established norms and creating a coalition. Affect, as an element of transnational assemblages, could be the perception of a situation that leads to a modification of the body, which then triggers the emotion of consciousness of the mind (Deleuze and Guattari, as cited in Papacharissi). Such consciousness triggered by the need to go against the colonial rule created a political response in Puerto Rican communities.

Sometimes, the desire to act immediately in response to affect and to stand up to ineffective practices comes in the form of a social media post. One participant shared that she used her Facebook, Twitter, and Instagram accounts to share news, her opinions on politics, and so on. In using these mediums, she would criticize the governmental disaster aid practices and the US government. Not only did this space became a source of information for people, this space also became a space for people to come together to share similar anger and resentment toward the malpractices that were occurring in the aftermath of Hurricane Maria. During the disaster, this participant's social media accounts became a source of information for people who followed her. Through her social media accounts and her work on the radio, the participant was able to create a network of journalists around Puerto Rico that helped to provide accurate and instant information to their viewers and listeners. Using their writing and information-gathering capacities, some participants who were journalists took to their social media accounts to communicate with the diaspora that wanted to communicate, receive updates about the situation, and help. This meant that through personal social media accounts, journalists were creating transnational assemblages with people outside of Puerto Rico and inviting them to respond to the disaster or participate in the discourse of disaster. Much of those conversations were about coloniality and criticizing the governments.

Social media platforms additionally provided Puerto Ricans with an assortment of tools to further their disaster response goals. Another participant, for example, noted the innovative use of Facebook in his university class that led him and his students to organize a relief campaign on the platform. The participant shared that while he was organizing the relief, he used Facebook Live, the platform's livestreaming feature, to showcase accountability, and he used WhatsApp's group chat function to communicate with his relief team. Yet another participant described how they used their Facebook accounts and GoFundMe pages to fundraise, and they used Amazon's Wish List feature, which allows users to create a virtual shopping list of items they need, to request the necessary relief materials. These fundraising activities requested housing materials such as solar panels and lamps, food, and immediate relief materials. Many other participants also mentioned that they used the Amazon Wish List feature to collect donations that helped people. Various smaller organizations, local people, and members of the Puerto Rican diaspora were involved in the relief efforts. Two participants, who initiated their relief actions via Facebook, received a great amount of support and donations, allowing them to formally establish a nonprofit organization that provides reconstruction supplies and other support to people who were affected by the calamity. In this way, various technologies and their affordances were being used to organize social actions via transnational assemblages. The use of very private spaces to do public work and to do a better job than the government showcases disaster response as a political act that was not just disaster response but also an action against the colonial ignorance of the US government and the Puerto Rican local government.

To further illustrate how private spaces are used to complete public work during a crisis, a participant representing a very popular community-based organization in Puerto Rico shared that their organization was able to help people communicate with their loved ones by providing community members with access to their satellite phones, internet services, and local radio station. This showcases self-sufficiency and non-reliance on the technologies of larger organizations or the government to satisfy the needs of the people, another decolonial action which aims at creating an equitable society. One of the needs of the people during Hurricane Maria was the need to communicate with their loved ones and to know that they were okay. The participant recounts:

> So there were sometimes 200 people making a line to use the phone to communicate with the people in the state, outside [of] Puerto Rico, and also from other parts of the island. (Participant from Puerto Rico)

My participant's organization was also able to raise the funds necessary to provide alternative sources of energy to people living in very geographically secluded locations. The participant recalled that people from many countries pledged monetary and material support (like satellite phones) to the organization because they trusted it.

While addressing inequalities in disaster response efforts and challenging colonial practices and local government inaction, Puerto Rican participants formed transnational assemblages by relying on various social media platforms and technologies. Such actions decolonized disaster response by decentering the relief from the local and the US government's control and focusing on social justice for the community. The participants used assorted technological mediums that ranged from their mobile phones and laptops to the internet to create space, channels, and transnational assemblages that supported suffering communities via a decolonial praxis motivated by a sense of responsibility. Puerto Ricans' use of social media was significant because it became an outlet for people to express their frustrations, curate information, join existing networks or form their own networks, and, most important, discuss social injustices and come together to face such injustices. Soto Vega believes that this use of social media acts as a resistance against the governmental norms. Such resistance was seen through how Puerto Ricans mobilized the technologies at their disposal to assert themselves, to conduct disaster response, and to challenge the governmental aid distribution practices and the indifference of the US government. Hence, the formation of the transnational assemblages was a way that not only represented rhetorical agency, but it also represented resistance, both of which constitute the decolonial praxis of disaster response.

## ENACTING CRISIS COMMUNICATION WITH SOCIAL JUSTICE DURING HURRICANE MARIA

Social media platforms became a place where Puerto Ricans could control their own narratives. Such narratives helped in the enactment of crisis communication with a social justice framework during Hurricane Maria. Participants shared that they curated the information on their respective Facebook accounts and websites and shared it with their community to help them. Social media became an important platform where crisis publics could seek, share, interpret, and disperse information to their networks to create a real-time awareness of what is going on and inviting people to join forces together for socially just disaster response. In seeking and gathering the information, crisis publics become part of various transnational assemblages. This variety of flows of crisis communications played an important part in the formation of transnational assemblage. In performing these crisis communications during the emergency within their assemblages and beyond, the actors responded to the disaster. As articulated by the participants who did not represent any organizations, their communication was not moderated by any organizational protocol. However, crisis communications within transnational assemblages were oriented toward gathering truthful information, verifying that information with the community, and using it to work toward providing disaster relief to the community with grounding on social justice. An activist participant from Puerto Rico shared:

> We're not going to manipulate the information. We're not going to make it look better or worse, so somebody gets the money. We are completely transparent, completely, like I said before, for the people, by the people. We have no agenda. Our only agenda is to give a voice to those people that don't have a voice. That's different. I didn't know this, but humanitarian relief is very profitable, extremely profitable. (Participant from Puerto Rico)

As the participant noted, Puerto Ricans decolonized knowledge production and dissemination. The activists and disaster responders demanded transparency in information, and local community-based organizations were the ones who were strongly advocating for such information, which the colonial rulers were either hiding or not sharing.

Local community-based organizations and activists served as a communication channel between local advocates and Puerto Ricans in the diaspora. They used the internet and physical spaces to collect donations while also serving as a hub for building community and ensuring survival (Soto Vega). Platforms like Facebook were used by various Puerto Ricans in the United States and around the globe to respond to Hurricane Maria in a truthful and real manner and in a way that challenged the traditional or official ways of disaster response. As my participant suggests, there was a lot of information manipulation that occurred during the crisis. According to the participants, the honesty of the people using these platforms is what made them become the reliable source of information within their community, and that allowed them to become a powerful voice to challenge the colonial consequences and disparities. Participants recognized their use of social media, journalism, or organizational platforms to perform crisis communication. They articulated the need for and importance of communication during the time of disaster not only to decentralize aid, but also to speak out against injustices, very similar to the Nepali community. A representative of a community-based organization shared that, to collect data and information about the community, they had to conduct interviews with the community members by talking to them one-on-one. This was because the resilient culture of the Puerto Rican community would prevent the survivors from sharing their difficulties. Actors therefore needed to change their practices because community members who were in shock were not opening up and were hiding their emotions and feelings due to the psychological trauma of the hurricane.

Participants who were journalists mainly working through official news channels and who were involved in writing, reporting, photographing, and broadcasting 24/7 during Hurricane Maria articulated how the disaster allowed them to think and act differently. They expressed how they wanted to highlight more marginalized voices, the governmental atrocities, and how colonial practices had impacted the community. They moved beyond their jobs and started using their social media platforms to emphasize photographs and videos that created awareness of what was really happening as opposed to solely reporting what the government was presenting. It was important for all these journalists to write, publish, and share factual stories about what was going on in Puerto Rico, specifically in US-based media. These journalists needed to rethink communication during a crisis, and they needed to think about how they could write in a way that put people's needs above all else while also sharing truthful information. The journalists' affective response of sharing information and equally criticizing the government, dismantling misinformation, and providing a space for marginalized voices in the written or audio-video communication they created moved them from being regular journalists to being an outlet for political decolonial action against common Western media practices.

One of the most amazing works done to decolonize information while all systems of communication were down in Puerto Rico was that accomplished by a radio station called WAPA Radio. This was the only radio station that was functioning throughout the island after the hurricane made landfall, and the station owners themselves continued to broadcast 24/7, relaying news and information as much as they could. One of my journalist participants shared that they were listening to this radio station. When they recognized that the same people were constantly broadcasting, they decided to go to the radio station with coffee and sandwiches. When the broadcasters saw my participant, they invited my participant to broadcast the news. Aside from being the major source of information for much of Puerto Rico, this station eventually became a relief hub that people relied on during and after Hurricane Maria. My participant shared:

> I said on air, "All the reporters, I know there's not going to be any newspapers or any television or radio stations working. So, if you have nothing to do, please come. We need your help. This is the only network that is operating, and we need to help them. They don't have any employees, and this is the only way. . . . . We have to do our community service." So, about 70 reporters and former reporters showed up, and we created a schedule. (Participant from Puerto Rico)

This announcement was crucial because it was a call that evoked emotions, an affective call that drove 70 reporters to show up and do what they could. Rather than a cry *for* help, this was an invitation for people *to* help. Through the radio, the participant was able to project the voices of people who were suffering and help them connect to the appropriate disaster responders. While working at WAPA Radio, the participant also used her social media accounts to make the communication process more dynamic and to reach people outside of Puerto Rico.

In Hurricane Maria's case, smaller community-based organizations, churches, private organizations, and organizations like the American Red Cross were more active than larger international humanitarian organizations. The role of the community-based organizations was larger in that they knew the needs and requirements of the community they were working for, and they understood their audiences well. As in Nepal, larger humanitarian organizations in Puerto Rico were also criticized for manipulating information and not being held accountable for spreading misinformation. Because having accurate information was very crucial during the disaster, participants articulated that they relied on information shared on Facebook by friends and family members as opposed to that shared by official organizations. One participant who represented a community-based organization that worked in disaster response shared the following:

> The one thing that I've found is that information is power, and people don't want to give up their power. Bigger humanitarian relief organizations feel threatened by open platforms like ours because, I'm not saying the Red Cross, but somebody like the Red Cross that has its platform. They have private platforms, and they have access and power. After all, they have the numbers, and they'll get money because they have this information that nobody else has. What we're doing is we're democratizing, or whatever the word is, the information so the government cannot manipulate the data. It's completely transparent. If there are 20 sick people, it's going to be on our website. (Participant from Puerto Rico)

Grassroots organizations and community organizers challenged the national narrative shared by the government and by other large humanitarian organizations. This decolonial act of challenge further supported the community because it sought out factual information from the community and, in turn, provided the community with accurate information regarding aid and its distribution. This also helped a lot of volunteers and donors to serve the community in need. Grassroots organizations therefore challenged governmental narratives and provided accurate information for people. This decentralizing of information was one of the major aspects of decolonial disaster response as information is power and that power can be used to challenge the government norms.

## CONCLUSION: DECOLONIAL DISASTER RESPONSE

During Hurricane Maria, Puerto Ricans created alternative processes for giving and receiving aid. Puerto Ricans also developed cross-diasporic communicative opportunities, a situation significant for supporting vulnerable communities to survive. Using social media for decolonial activism is not a new thing in Puerto Rico (Soto Vega). Hurricane Maria caused a lot of communication disruptions. But when the US government was very silent on disaster aid and relief, and the protocols, rules, and regulations established to respond to calamities created circumstances where the disaster aids were stuck at the ports and people were losing their lives, Puerto Ricans still responded. My participants shared that they invested themselves, their time, and their energy in a way that allowed them to respond to the catastrophe by creating their own disaster response mechanism, by gathering resources from their communities across the world, and by communicating Puerto Ricans' needs despite the communication disruption created by the disaster. The decolonial ways of communication and disaster response, as opposed to Western aid practices, had the purpose of serving the community, providing access to aid, and acting as a voice for the marginalized populations who were suffering. There was a display of distrust in the US government and the Puerto Rican government as it lacked community care or knowledge of how people's lives had been affected by the hurricane. Moreover, the colonial practices that involved protocols and delay in decision-making were not helpful for the Puerto Rican community. Puerto Ricans were voicing their displeasure against the US government's colonial rhetoric. The decolonial disaster response described by the Puerto Rican participants could be summarized as such:

- **Autogestión:** The Puerto Rican community displayed *autogestión* as a coalitional counter-praxis of survival (Soto Vega) where people were creating spaces for healing and communal support when the state had not provided one. By displaying this survival praxis, Puerto Ricans were building community across the borders via transnational assemblages and ensuring that those who needed support got that support.

- **Community Values:** A lot of Puerto Rican participants displayed values of courage and dedication to their community during the aftermath of Hurricane Maria. They were empathetic toward their community and had a sense of responsibility toward their people, which motivated them to become involved in disaster response efforts. Community-level actions were fundamental to restoring access to neighborhoods and, ultimately, saving lives (Rodríguez-Díaz).
- **Resistance and Agency:** The participants shared their resistance against the governmental system and agency. Lloréns and Santiago argue that a lot of women were involved in the disaster response efforts (a conclusion that I reached as well). Through their solidarity, mutual help, and support, these women were involved in community initiatives which could be argued to be forms of resistance and agency (Lloréns and Santiago 402). Such strategies of resistance countered the governmental mismanagement, thus resulting in "radical forms of decentralized resistance to state disinvestment and resource extraction" (Soto Vega 45). These forms of resistance were supported by actors engaging with whatever the community needed the very moment it was needed.
- **Disaster Activism:** The decolonial approach to disaster response in Puerto Rico was also characterized by activism and equity. This activism/decolonial approach was focused on making sure that the disaster response was conducted with dignity and put the community needs first, while the US and Puerto Rican government ignored these needs. Furthermore, such activism also showcased courage, empathy, and motivation toward supporting the community. Some examples of activism included reaching out to the community to understand what aid was needed, providing immediate relief, and clearing blocked roads. The disaster activism was not limited to Puerto Rico itself; it also expanded across national and geographical boundaries.

In this chapter, I showcased autógestion as a praxis used by Puerto Ricans to respond to and resist the devastating aftermath of Hurricane Maria and the response by the US government. Like the Nepalis, Puerto Ricans created transnational connections and formed various transnational assemblages motivated by autógestion. As articulated previously, the decolonial disaster response was displayed by the intersection of the following: a sense of community, resistance and agency, disaster activism, and autógestion. With this autógestion as a praxis, the participants launched multiple disaster response efforts via transnational assemblages that helped and supported the community when they were in need. Such assemblages were created to raise funds, send materials, organize relief, and create connections with the people. Finally, as with the Nepal earthquake, the disaster response by Puerto Ricans demonstrates that local disasters are global concerns and handling and responding to such disasters requires a larger transnational network that is grounded in social justice actions.

# 4

## Social Justice–Oriented Technical Communications in Global Disaster Management

Global engagement during a disaster is made possible with the formation of transnational assemblages that create space to acknowledge and support suffering marginalized communities. As such, the transnational assemblages' actions and engagements are crucial for global disaster management because they allow for social justice-oriented communication which supports the most vulnerable communities around the globe. As I showcased, transnational assemblages, coalition forming, and digital actions are inevitable during a disaster, and I have chosen to examine the use of social media by disaster responders in performing such actions. With this demonstration, I argue that there is an urgency for both rhetoric and technical communication as a field to explore how the global technical communications praxis helps to address injustices in a contemporary networked world. I further this argument to illustrate how rhetoric and technical communication scholars can perform transdisciplinary research in disaster management to minimize the impacts of catastrophic disasters affecting the world's most vulnerable populations. I conclude that intersectionality and a social justice framework will help contextualize information based on the local circumstances, exposing the potential places where marginalization may occur.

This chapter will describe ways to identify and work with the differing transnational assemblages, create strategies to work with community organizers, and lead disaster response efforts by putting the local knowledge at the center of each endeavor. I end with practical solutions where I depict some approaches for developing social justice-oriented technical communication. Finally, I address the need for future studies and suggest how scholars may incorporate this research in various university courses.

## DISASTER RESPONSE IN A GLOBALIZED WORLD

It is important to emphasize that the response to a local disaster is not limited to local people or international humanitarian organizations. Disaster response in a globalized world is global, digital, and comprised of the global actors who are from unofficial public spheres. In a catastrophic situation, disaster response efforts are very chaotic and continue to grow and expand based on the need of the people or the organization. Disaster also initiates transnational assemblage where responders (people or organizations) depend on various technologies such as mobile phones, the internet, and social media to motivate a common disaster response. Crisis communication in such assemblages helps to facilitate communications among various actors. Mapping the network, understanding the places where disaster response is happening, and recognizing how communication is moving will serve in easing disaster response efforts. In mapping a disaster network, various actors become involved: disaster relief groups, volunteers, donors, medical service providers, engineers, community leaders, humanitarian organizations, and governments, for example. These actors may work individually within their own assemblages or connect with other transnational assemblages to seek or provide support. Additionally, the use of digital technologies made it easier for the actors to connect and work together and respond to disasters.

The transnational assemblages that were formed during the Nepal earthquake and Hurricane Maria were motivated by affect and supported by social media in the form of information, pictures, hashtags, or online communities. People's interactions on Twitter during the two disasters transformed the Twittersphere into an updated information-providing platform that allowed easy access not just for people, but also for governments, volunteers, different aid agencies, and organizations. Transnational assemblages have a social and political impact and could really do significant work during a time of disaster, as I demonstrated in this book. As more users around the globe have made social media a part of their lives, the role of social media platforms in disaster response efforts will likely be even more prominent (Kim and Hastak; Potts et al.). The formation of transnational assemblages via digital activism displayed by people using social media in Nepal and Puerto Rico has undeniably helped communities and people who are in need, even though these users mostly provided information which led to the communities receiving various aids to survive. Twitter aided the disaster response efforts by bringing people from around the world together to form transnational assemblages that are emerging and autonomous in pursuing a common response to the disaster. They are non-hierarchical and are welcoming to anyone who wants to be a part of such an organized space (Marcus and Saka). Additionally, these assemblages are powerful because they challenge authorities or governments or news media and work toward the greater good of the community. As I have demonstrated, where the Nepali and Puerto Rican governments could not reach, the transnational assemblages reached, and where justice failed, transnational assemblages asserted themselves to create an inclusive space that fought for justice.

During a disaster, transnational assemblages act autonomously and encompass the rhetorical agency of humans who are supported by non-human elements, such as mobile phones, the internet, laptops, relief materials, food, and medical services. That is why the impact of digital technologies in the disaster response is very apparent as per the case studies discussed previously. In detaching themselves from one whole and assembling into another, the rhetorical agency of each assemblage plays a vital role. Amy Koerber defines rhetorical agency as "negotiation among competing alternative discourses, that grants individuals some ability to reject discursive elements that they find problematic" (94). Both Nepalis and Puerto Ricans did not abide by the narratives that the government, the media, and the larger humanitarian organizations were promoting. Rather, they were listening closely to their communities and knew that their communities required more support than what the official narratives believed and propagated. Nepalis' and Puerto Ricans' self-organized transnational assemblages embodied rhetorical agency by displaying what Natasha N. Jones in her article "Rhetorical Narratives of Black Entrepreneurs . . ." refers to as "a) an awareness of the rhetorical situation, including exigency, Kairos, and an understanding of existing discourses or arguments, and b) the ability, opportunity, or rhetorical space to act" (325). Such self-organization in both disasters was quicker, more efficient, and more effective due to the space provided by digital technologies to exercise agency, conduct discourses, and initiate disaster relief actions. Hence, digital technologies have a greater role and importance in the context of large-scale disasters.

Transnational assemblages embody the characteristics of becoming and the constant process of transformation (Slack and Wise), which is why, as the disaster situation emerges, the response systems and these assemblages also emerge. Disaster responders, actors, volunteers, and organizations can continue to monitor the transformation as these assemblages keep growing, transforming, or shrinking based on the needs and requirements of the post-disaster context. As I have demonstrated, transnational assemblages during a catastrophic disaster involve actors who live locally or globally, who are engaged within the local spaces, or who have ties to the local spaces. Therefore, as these transnational assemblages emerge globally, they could utilize the existing and new spaces by forging newer articulations, such as creating physical spaces or, in the present context, creating spaces on the web or other internet-based platforms. These assemblages could also establish member roles or the elements of the assemblages (DeLanda; Slack and Wise). Transnational assemblages evolve to achieve objectives or certain tasks; however, those tasks are under constant modifications based on the shifting demands, which is why spontaneous actions and decision-making happen. In this process, sometimes in the process of formation the elements of assemblages might become disconnected and may lose their relevance or become less influential. These transnational assemblages are motivated by affect and possess agency to respond to a global phenomenon like a disaster. They occupy spaces via digital mediums where pictures, videos, and texts, embedded in the form of information, create an intense action that motivates various actors and elements of the assemblage to act.

During both the Nepal and Puerto Rico disasters, social media became an important platform where crisis publics could seek, share, interpret, and disperse information to their networks and create a community to challenge the ongoing injustices and socio-political dilemmas. In seeking and gathering the information, crisis publics became part of various transnational assemblages that worked together to challenge the socio-political systems of oppressions that created obstructions during these two disasters. These crisis publics who emerge during a disaster might not follow official protocols that might lead to quick decision-making. Social media also allowed crisis publics to perform crisis communications within their assemblages, as suggested by Finn Frandsen and Winni Johansen by a) communicating to each other, b) communicating with each other, c) communicating against each other or the official narratives shared by the government, d) communicating past each other, and e) communicating about each other

(433). This variety of crisis communication flows played an important part in conducting activism on multiple platforms and evoking emotions that motivated people to take part in disaster relief efforts. Communication flows allowed these transnational assemblages to continue to grow and make an impact on the political level. As articulated by the participants in my study who did not represent any organizations, their communication was not moderated by any organizational protocol. However, crisis communications within their own assemblages were oriented toward gathering truthful information, verifying it with the community, and using that information to work toward providing disaster relief to the community.

As my results demonstrated, communication during a crisis can be enhanced through digital technologies and social media because they allow for quicker delivery of information to a larger public. With access to various technological tools, as Liza Potts argues in *Social Media in Disaster Response*, technology experts and scientists could work hand in hand with social scientists, including technical communicators, to respond more effectively to crises. The rhetorical situation of each disaster is different, and it presents unique challenges in communication. In the crisis situations created by the two disasters I have addressed, communications were mediated by official and unofficial organizations through self-organized crisis publics in transnational assemblages. The formation of transnational assemblages in the digital web facilitated communications by building "a series of locality-based activities and organizations around a key function in the network" (Castells 443). These transnational assemblages composed of crisis publics helped in spreading urgent messages that informed audiences, making people aware of the situation, and encouraging precautionary measures.

## SOCIAL JUSTICE-ORIENTED TECHNICAL COMMUNICATION IN DISASTER RESPONSE

It is important to emphasize that we continue to live through compounding crises and disasters. Thus, we should understand that without social justice at the core of disaster response and communication, we will continue to lose lives and create harm to suffering communities. We must also understand that various catastrophic events establish differing rhetorical situations, which is contextual to the place, time, people, culture, histories, and socio-political situation of the affected communities. As Haas and Eble remind us, "Social justice approaches to technical communication are often informed by cultural theories and methodologies, but they also explicitly seek to redistribute and reassemble—or otherwise redress—power imbalances that systematically and systemically disenfranchise some stakeholders while privileging others" (4). Hence, social justice-oriented technical communication in disaster response will help in challenging the unequal systems of power that mobilize during a disaster and provide grounding and flexibility to address changed newer forms of socially unjust situations created by disasters. Disasters are a geopolitical issue, and Dinesh Paudel and Gregory Reck argue that the current structure of the global system governed by global capital based on geopolitical inequities and unequal systems of power creates varying levels of vulnerability, including those relevant to disasters (n.p.). For example, one community receiving more relief because of their "visibility" while others are ignored because of their "invisibility" constitutes an unjust situation (Cedillo). The COVID-19 pandemic, the Russia-Ukraine war, and the Gaza war are yet other examples where we see and experience how inequalities, injustices, and biases are manifested in disaster response and management efforts. However, as I have showcased in previous chapters, people do respond to such situations affectively by sharing their lived experiences and those of others through the assorted modes of communication and by actively working to respond to disaster situations. For example, in the cases of Nepal and Puerto Rico, transnational assemblages emerged as a powerful force that challenged the established systems, norms, and policies and moved beyond geographies to support the most vulnerable populations.

By grounding their work in non-Western and decolonial values, the participants motivated by affective reactions were able to articulate the injustices affecting the damaged communities, revealing those injustices on social media platforms, and calling people to take action to reject such injustices. They also collaborated transnationally to form coalitions to tackle such injustices (Walton et al.). In both disasters, the communications and work distribution within various transnational assemblages helped in forming alliances or coalitions that became a larger assemblage (e.g., a social justice movement), which created social justice goals for disaster response efforts (DeLanda). These goals were achieved by implementing a disaster response effort informed by a) non-Western and decolonial practices and b) affective dimensions of the experiences of the marginalized and vulnerable populations living through social injustices. These practices of affectively helping a community spontaneously allowed the participants to create transnational connections that further helped communities in need.

Based on my participants' narratives, I define the non-Western and decolonial ways of crisis communication in the context of the Nepal earthquake and Hurricane Maria as alternative crisis communication performed by individuals unrelated to any official or international organizations to curate, share, and validate information for the larger public by using varied publicly accessible digital technologies and platforms. Nepalis and Puerto Ricans were using various social media platforms for networking and sharing information during both disasters; they were also using social media platforms for non-Western and decolonial disaster response claiming social media space as their own to conduct crisis communications. The creation of alternative processes for giving and receiving aid, in addition to cross-diasporic communicative opportunities, were significant for decentralizing the aid in Puerto Rico and also in Nepal. Crisis communication during a disaster should be practiced with social justice at the core of its purpose, highlighting and voicing the experiences of marginalized and vulnerable communities. In the aftermath of both disasters, the actors who were involved in crisis communication were focused on uplifting communities, helping people in need, and creating alternative spaces for people to voice their concerns and opinions.

By understanding the work of the transnational assemblages' crisis communication and distributed work practices, scholars, practitioners, policymakers, and technical and professional communication (TPC) teachers can work toward developing stronger mechanisms to understand people's vulnerabilities during a disaster. Allowing communication during a crisis to be shaped by affective dimensions of people's lived experiences will help in mitigating the challenges of the disaster via social justice-oriented crisis communication and distributed work. It is important for practitioners, researchers, and disaster responders who dedicate their life and work to responding to emergencies to adjust crisis communication toward ending social injustices. Furthermore, while performing any kind of disaster response, the cultural context, and issues of injustices within such contexts of the affected space should be taken into consideration. Without such adaptation, there is a danger of further amplifying social injustices. Technical communication scholars, practitioners, and teachers are powerful information and communication mediators during any kind of crisis. As experts in communicating complex information, disaster researchers and crisis communicators can collaboratively work with engineers and scientists to design a social justice-oriented disaster response effort (Baniya, "How Technical Communicators"). Such a social justice-oriented disaster response effort could ground the actors' work in understanding the cultural, social, political, and economic intersections of the affected community. In the following sections, I present the ways in which social justice-oriented disaster response efforts can be designed in diverse spaces.

### Intersectionality in Disaster Response

Disaster response in the current context can be a social action. Such response should be grounded in an intersectional perspective such that disaster responders understand how risk, adaptability, social vulnerability, and historical injustice intersect with each other and how they marginalize people with certain identities. The participants I have interviewed suggest that they witnessed institutional inequalities in disaster response and aid distribution efforts that privileged one group or community and discriminated against others. Hence, incorporating an intersectional perspective in disaster response efforts allows the responders to get a deeper understanding of how systemic violence and discrimination are rooted and how such discrimination manifests itself during the aftermath of a disaster. This approach also allows the disaster responders to understand that there is an interconnection of people, social problems, and ideas (Collins; Crenshaw). This approach further brings together ideas from disparate places, times, and perspectives and enables people to share points of view that were formerly forbidden, outlawed, or simply obscured (Collins). This approach is very important when responding to a disaster because "disaster response" is a social action and intersectionality helps in redefining what such social action could look like. Such social action could mean that we take race, gender, caste system, and other social hierarchies into account because often, such social hierarchies become the determining factors of who bears the brunt of emergencies and who is the last to recover from such calamities (Klopp et al).

### Understanding the Role of Local and Global Actors within Transnational Assemblages

The work of actors who emerge during a disaster is dynamic, powerful, and social justice-oriented. Hence, the major disaster responders need to identify those actors and understand their work within the transnational assemblages. Doing so can lead to faster disaster response and recovery. As I have mentioned time and again, local disasters become global concerns, and there is an emergence of countless actors both locally and globally. Observing and becoming aware of the formation of such groups of actors will help in mobilizing people to support the vulnerable communities. Various transnational assemblages perform crisis communication via distributed work to ensure social justice, which helps contextualize information based on the local context. Therefore, larger organizations with resources should work collaboratively with these emerging actors to move toward understanding the issues of social justice and to collectively attempt to solve such concerns during a disaster. Spaces like social media platforms play a prominent role in disaster response efforts, a role that should be enhanced with the lessons from past disasters. Practitioners and researchers should work together to develop a mechanism that allows actors to connect with multiple transnational assemblages to tackle the consequences of a disaster.

### Honoring Local Knowledges and Practices

Finally, in disaster response, it is often the case that local knowledge and practices are not listened to and honored as the chaotic situation creates imbalances in power structure. While, in writing a lot of times, it is said that we have to honor local knowledges and practices, in actual situation of disaster, this is something that is overlooked. When that happens, there will be a mismatch between what the community needs and what aid communities actually receive. Disaster responders, researchers, and practitioners should honor the people from vulnerable spaces and people with marginalized identities. Listening to the stories of struggle, historical marginalization, and how such marginalization creates newer forms of inequities should be discussed openly with the community. The affective responses of the local community during disasters should be considered while communicating and researching crises as doing so acknowledges the lived experiences, values, and suffering of the affected community. This means that while conducting disaster response, community-based knowledge should be part of the planning and response efforts because without community knowledge and without honoring the community practices, the effects of compounding disasters cannot be averted quickly. Organizations can collaborate with various actors from transnational assemblages who have experiences of collaborating with the community. This will help in creation of a committee where community leaders are in consultation and will help brainstorming issues and solutions to those problems in a way that honors the community's identity and practices.

## PRACTICAL SOLUTIONS: HOW CAN TECHNICAL COMMUNICATORS SUPPORT DISASTER RESPONSE?

Crisis communications conducted by crisis publics via transnational assemblages can facilitate disaster response because they convey messages and share information through multiple channels of communication, such as mobile phones, SMS, emails, tweets, and Facebook and WhatsApp messages. These messages include information regarding the need for relief materials, calls for volunteers, and requests for funding, which can be regarded as the "flows in an assemblage" (DeLanda). The communication performed by the crisis publics during both the Nepal and Puerto Rico disasters provided a public voice for communities who were being ignored. Such communications were flexible, adaptive, and did not have any official protocols. While repurposing such messages with social media functions like sharing, retweeting, liking, replying, and sometimes rewriting and translating, the crisis communication practices during these two crises blurred the boundaries between the official and unofficial networks. Crisis communications are mostly employed in an organizational context (Walaski); however, my data suggests that because the context of the world is continuously evolving during a crisis (for example number of casualties or any new information about crisis), hence, crisis communication is also always transforming. In this context, catastrophic disasters invite multiple stakeholders, organizations, and several evolving assemblages to communicate about the crisis and the aid necessary to ease the disaster response efforts. To manage a successful disaster response, stronger crisis communication mechanisms that involve and highlight the role of the community and the people who are affected by disaster response efforts are required (Coombs and Holladay; Horsley and Barker; Walaski).

The suffering and need during catastrophic disasters create a chaotic situation which generates communication crises as people begin seeking information, with many individuals and organizations emerging who curate and share information. Potts (*Social Media in Disaster Response*) argues that people need information immediately, so they dig through the entire system to find that information. They communicate and reach out to other people who might have expertise or who might be a reliable source of information. During the first weeks after the disaster events, the Nepal earthquake and Hurricane Maria changed the dynamics and the rhetorical nature of crisis communication. The public moved from being passive receivers of crisis communication to becoming active responders, interpreters, and transmitters of information (Coombs and Holladay). These active roles, as my analysis of the narratives suggests, allowed the actors to take on prominent roles in decentralizing communication on social medial platforms, as "the decentralized communications structure in most social media means that these platforms provide different communicative affordances during disasters" (Murthy and Gross 357). This can be seen in actors' interpretations of messages, individual expressions, and criticisms of official organizations. During a time of a disaster, digital tools empower local people's voices more so than they do those of professional communicators of major media outlets (Frost).

We now know that crisis communication during a disaster is multidimensional and involves various official and unofficial actors. Technical communicators can play a greater role to provide accurate information and tackle misinformation by working closely with experts, scientists, journalists, and other officials. To take on the consequences of any disaster, collaborative work is essential. This sort of collaborative work in the digital age takes the form of transnational assemblages that incorporate transcultural communities who are spread across the world and time zones, but who come together to face the consequences of a disaster, which can be regarded as "distributed work" (Pigg). To address injustices during or after a crisis, professional communicators have a civic responsibility in ensuring equity and justice. In the following sections, I present specific recommendations for technical communicators based on the results of my study and my discussion.

## Transnational Crisis Publics

This project has showcased the work of transnational crisis publics for social justice. As I described in the introduction and illustrated throughout the book, transnational crisis publics emerge from often ignored spaces to support marginalized communities as communicators and advocates during a disaster. Handling catastrophic disasters and crises requires careful consideration of communities, their suffering, and their contexts. In this chaotic context, transnational crisis publics emerge to facilitate crisis communication in their respective communities and challenge the privileged narratives. The rhetorical agency of the transnational crisis publics as well as how they come together to negotiate power and privilege to challenge the systems of oppression needs to be recognized. In a chaotic situation, larger crisis-handling organizations need to identify the emerging and emergent ever-changing various transnational crisis publics. They need to understand that crisis public interactions are non-static, that they blur the boundaries of local and global, official, and unofficial rhetorics. It is imperative that we understand the interconnectedness created via transnational assemblages to better understand the deep-rooted intricacies that any disaster might unravel. Technical communicators can help identify such transnational crisis publics and create a channel of communication via which a partnership can be forged for responding to the crisis.

## Context- and Culture-Specific Crisis Communication

Crisis communication has changed over the past 40 years. Such communications emerge during crises that are becoming increasingly global as their causes and consequences transcend national and cultural boundaries (Schwarz et al.). I have argued that Western knowledge-making practices may create difficulties in facilitating communication in the current risk or crisis environments (Boiarsky) because of a lack of a) contextual local knowledge, b) awareness of audience needs and requirements, and c) understanding of social justice and intercultural communications practices (Jones et al.). Hence, technical communicators who have a strong background in understanding context, audiences, and intercultural communication can support crisis communication efforts through providing context- and culture-specific crisis communication. Even though this audience-specific or cultural-specific communication is not new in the field, sometimes while communicating during a crisis, this gets ignored, and context-specific disaster response and communication don't happen. Hence, this is a reminder to various technical communicators and disaster responders that in any disaster-specific situation, context and culture need to be taken into consideration. This can happen in multiple different ways such as using local languages, cultural and contextual symbols, and representation of the local community and their knowledge in the communications materials produced. Utilizing the knowledge of document design and ability to communicate complex information to the public, technical communicators can help people who are suffering to get exact information that they need based on the context of the community.

### Crisis Communication for Social Justice

Crisis communications should incorporate a social justice framework that can support the marginalized and vulnerable communities affected by disasters (Walton et al.). Communications in such circumstances should be understood from a perspective that focuses on the receiver and represents the various voices of the marginalized population. As such, communications should not privilege one single voice, such as that of the government or a larger non-governmental organization (NGO). Crisis communication should help in making the communication effective during the disaster. Thus, technical communicators should become advocates for incorporating social justice-oriented crisis communication into disaster response efforts where they can specifically understand the ways in which marginalization happens in post-disaster situations and investigate the newer forms of social injustices that could happen (Walton et al.). Technical communicators can play a vital role in communicating during disaster with social justice by determining how various transnational assemblages are constructed, how various other networks of distribution of aid and information are formed and by whom, toward what ends, as well as the stakeholders, power dynamics, distributed agency, and directions of the material and information flows within the networks (Haas and Eble 4). Lastly, technical communicators can establish coalitions by working together with community-based organizers or the transnational assemblages themselves to create a space for advocacy.

### Representing Community Voices in Crisis Communication

Technical communicators should explore, investigate, and challenge practices that marginalize their targeted audiences within their respective institutions and during the situations of a disaster (Walton et al.; Ding). While working in a high-pressure environment and situation like a crisis, technical communicators should really represent the voices of a community that is suffering. Rose et al. remind us that developing collaboration embedded in community helps in trust and access to community members and creates an easier pathway to serve them. Technical communicators can collaborate with the community and work together to address the issues during a disaster. The situation of the catastrophe requires very sensitive and effective communication and a developed trust with the community because crisis changes the dynamics, needs, and reactions of the community that is suffering. One way to observe such dynamic communication, needs, and reactions is by observing social media platforms. Social media platforms create the possibility for understanding the public reaction to a disaster in real time, while also allowing for the emergence of crisis publics that embrace the role of disaster management (Murthy and Gross, Baniya "How Technical Communicators", Potts). Thus, social media can become a space where technical communicators can observe how crisis communication is happening within the communities, identify key actors or influencers, and work toward amplifying the voices of the people. TPC researchers can further explore ways of strengthening crisis communication mechanisms for a successful disaster response in non-Western and decolonial contexts, ones that foreground the role of the community and disaster responders, and ones that ensure social justice by voicing the concerns and opinions of the marginalized and vulnerable communities.

## PEDAGOGICAL INTERVENTIONS

Pedagogically, this research supports instructors who want to teach the conventions of TPC in transnational communication, research methodologies, and the rhetoric of disaster. In this regard, I would like to return to the argument about narrative and storytelling as an important aspect that can be taught within a classroom. Storytelling has been a major concept in cultural rhetoric and various indigenous rhetorics (King et al.; Powell). As Jacqueline Jones Royster argues, stories have the capacity to unmask truths as they have vital layers of the transformative process (35). Students can be taught to take up narrative and storytelling as a lesson in learning how to analyze and produce crisis communication in transnational contexts. In Appendix D, I share an example of a senior undergraduate-level capstone course called Disaster and Crisis Communication. In other courses, instructors who teach genres like research reports or white papers could incorporate disaster research into their assignments.

Specifically, an assignment could focus on researching a particular disaster and communication during that crisis with a focus on storytelling and narrative and producing specific products. This would allow students to think of the varieties of communication practices and technologies that were used to address the disaster. This assignment could also be expanded upon by incorporating digital communication and design (see assignment example in Appendix E) where students can work in groups to establish communication plans for addressing a crisis. Instructors could also create courses on topics such as rhetoric of disaster, transnational communication approaches, or mixed-methods research. An aspect of crisis or risk communication could be incorporated into service courses, such as business communication, technical writing, or rhetoric and writing courses that serve various departments in universities.

Service-learning or civic engagement courses could also be developed in partnership with local or international organizations or to help the students prepare for local and global risks. In these courses, students could gain experience working through various digital platforms, such as Slack, Google Docs, X (formerly Twitter), and Trello. Moreover, a service-learning course within the business or technical writing fields could focus on risk communication and/or risk assessment. The course could be developed in partnership with a community member and focus on the development of disaster preparedness materials, various user documents, grant writing, fundraising, and methods that the organization can use when responding to a disaster. This course could help students understand how risk or crisis is communicated in a workplace setting, and they could help community partners gain support to be prepared for any disaster or crisis. As my research demonstrates, various actors within the disaster emerge organically from within their societies; hence, our own students sitting in our classes may become key actors who respond to future disasters. As disaster concerns everyone and could affect anyone in countless different ways, preparing students to communicate ethically, transparently, and quickly during a disaster situation can also help to contribute to the disaster response.

## CONCLUSION

The global community is currently challenged by multiple disasters (including a global pandemic, multiple different wars). Technical and professional communication researchers and practitioners have a set of skills and knowledge in terms of writing, interdisciplinary collaboration, communication, and public engagement to support communities facing natural disasters. Such responses require collaborative work, and, in such collaboration, technical communicators can play a greater role that helps in making the communication systems flexible and adaptive. In turn, these systems can help save the lives of people who are suffering during and after a calamity. Such knowledge can be used in future research which explores the specific roles of technical communicators that respond to a crisis.

In my research, I have only focused on immediate disaster response. And, due to the scope of the research, I was only able to shine a spotlight on limited aspects of these two disasters. Several years later, Nepalis are still bearing the consequences of the Nepal earthquake, and Puerto Ricans are also still struggling to recover from Hurricane Maria while multiple crises have happened in between. Reconstruction activities are already often hampered by local and international politics, but now, people must respond to other setbacks, such as the COVID-19 pandemic, while they are still recovering from the previous disasters. For my research, I used Twitter data to represent the populations who are present on social media and have access to Twitter. Many of these actors may not have been physically impacted by the disasters, but collectively, they were in a position to respond to the disasters by forming or joining transnational assemblages with people who were physically impacted. Future researchers can focus on learning about the coping mechanisms developed in marginalized societies that have been traumatized. They might also examine how people recover and reconstruct their lives and communities after disasters.

The study of disaster and environmental crisis is a growing area. As the world continues to suffer from countless natural disasters and risks caused or intensified by climate change, researchers need to collaborate to mitigate the challenges put forth by disasters. In this way, governmental and non-governmental organizations can work with disaster researchers to enhance their communication and documentation practices. Researchers can focus on understanding the evolving communication practices during disasters and study how crisis communications can be enhanced with the support of technology during and after the disaster. Other potential areas of research in crisis communications could enhance our understanding of disaster philanthropy, social entrepreneurship in disaster zones, community-based disaster risk management, and user experience in disaster response mechanisms. Besides Nepal and Puerto Rico, there are other marginalized countries where people suffer from the consequences of climate change and natural disasters. Researchers can also expand the scope of their research to these areas. And ultimately, I argue, we might join our research to support the transnational assemblages working for justice.

In this book, I have established a rhetorical framework grounded in lived experiences and intersectionality that opens pathways to improving disaster response both locally and globally. As such, this book and this framework invite contributions from scholars by developing, creating, and transferring knowledge via writing and advocacy. I posit that prioritizing marginalized voices and their grounded knowledge, rhetorical agency, and coalitional networks will enhance disaster response, which is not a focus of many studies in humanities and rhetorical studies. As the world suffers through compounding disasters, scholars in a variety of humanities disciplines, including technical communication, history, social sciences, and philosophy, argue for transdisciplinary approaches to provide unique solutions to global issues. As rhetoric and technical communication scholars, we need to rethink how we can contribute to the frontline response during a disaster. We have now survived the deadliest pandemic in history, and simultaneously, all other disasters due to climate change haven't stopped. As a result, there is an urgency for our field to rethink how we speak to the broader world issues by capturing social, historical, cultural, and communicative perspectives during any kinds of disaster and by providing a rhetorical and humanistic approach to prepare people for future disasters. As rhetorical and technical communication scholars, we need to develop strategies to showcase and openly talk about systems of oppression, colonial issues, and how marginalized people resist those circumstances, and we need to weave those stories and lived experiences into our scholarship and represent them in academic and non-academic spaces. Hence, this book calls upon scholars and practitioners to think about how they can challenge the dominant narrative, intentionally seek marginalized perspectives, and privilege the voices of the world's most vulnerable and marginalized populations, who are affected by the consequences of any big or small disasters.

Crises will continue to upend our lives. This is a crucial time to rethink our scholarship and how our work can support raising awareness about issues of disasters, climate change, and equity. I call on scholars to reimagine the work of disaster response and crisis communication and to explore how such reimagination can benefit not only scholarly communities but also practitioners of disaster response, volunteers, governments, and grassroots organizers.

# Epilogue

As a first responder (in the form of journalist and communication practitioner) to the 2015 Nepal earthquake that killed more than 8,000 people, I witnessed discrepancies in disaster relief and crisis communication that led me to pursue a PhD focused on improving future responses to global challenges. In 2017, I observed a similar disparity in disaster response as Hurricane Maria devastated Puerto Rico. These transformative lived experiences created a scholarly trajectory for me focused on significant and evolving global challenges and disasters, such as earthquakes, climate change, pandemics, or war. Witnessing racial injustices, inequities, and misinformation during COVID-19, I continue to interrogate *how we can improve the human condition when the globe is shaken by crises such as COVID-19, climate change, war, misinformation, and aid discrepancies.* We need to create space for global communities facing disasters for humanists to glean insights from the experiences of these communities and to develop public interventions by empowering first responders to conduct disaster responses with social justice. This book is an attempt to do so as it showcased how disaster responders in Nepal and Puerto Rico enabled global philanthropic partnerships and engagements via digital technologies to launch social justice-oriented disaster responses. However, there is still much to do. As a field, we need to integrate our knowledge, practices, and lived experiences of the community toward ending disparities and empowering marginalized populations. As cliché as it sounds, how are we moving beyond our publications and projects that are mostly from the walls of academia? As the time demands, we need stronger investment from scholars in building community and enhancing technological infrastructures aiding communication and fostering global partnerships to support vulnerable communities facing issues of disasters, climate change, health, and environmental disparities.

# Appendix A

## Twitter Use Case Description Form

**Name:** Sweta Baniya, Purdue University
**Email:** baniya@purdue.edu
**Legal Entity Name (Please include Inc., LLC, Corp. etc.):** Purdue University
**Organization Website:** www.purdue.edu
**Organization's Twitter Handle:** @LifeatPurdue (@Sunkesharee)
**Company Headquarters/Billing Address:** Purdue University,
500 Oval Drive
Heavlion Hall 324,
West Lafayette 47906
**Company description, including industries served and customer locations:** Public University, serving education.
**Twitter Use Case Description:** In paragraph form, please provide a detailed description of how Twitter data will be used in your service. In your description, please include answers to the following questions:
**What is the purpose of your product or service?**
The core use of the case is for academic purposes only. Twitter APIs will only be used for academic research purposes. There are no profit-generating activities, but this academic research is a contribution to society.
**What will you deliver to your users/customers?**
Since this is a work without any profit of customers, there is no delivery to the customers.
**How do you intend to analyze Tweets, Twitter users, or their content?**
Twitter users will not be analyzed. Their identities will not be revealed in any case. If there is a chance that the identities of the Twitter users will be revealed, then all of them will be anonymized. My research has been approved by IRB at Purdue University. The research during the data collection as well as analysis will adhere to the IRB protocol that protects all the human subjects that are related with the research. For the analysis, I will be using "Social Network Analysis" via NVivo to generate networks to see how people have networked via Twitter. For this research, there will be analysis

of only the keywords, but not the whole tweet. The keywords will be used to analyze for example, how many people have used hashtag #NepalEarthquake or have used keywords like "relief," "rescue," "help," and "donate." Only the numerical value will be analyzed. The content of the Tweets, as well as the identities displayers such as photographs or location or personal details, will not be used.

For the purpose of sharing, the results of Social Network Analysis will be presented in the form of written publication - the first will be my dissertation project, the second will be publications, and the third will be conferences. These are purely academic audiences and thus, there will be no profit-making involved in this.

**How is Twitter data displayed to users of your product or service (e.g., will Tweets and content be displayed at row level or aggregated)?**

Like I have mentioned above, the exact content of the Tweets wouldn't be displayed. However, the content, if necessary to be displayed, will be done during classroom activities, conferences, and peer-reviewed academic publications. Again, the identity of Twitter accounts will not be disclosed. Any tweets that disclose personal details and information will not be used for the dissemination. This way, the information shared will be able to protect the identities of the people. The results of Social Network Analysis are displayed in the form of maps and charts and graphs - hence, there will not be any information that is related to the human subjects (Twitter users) displayed. Only the numbers will be displayed. Additionally, the research doesn't involve tweeting, retweeting, or liking the content, or interaction with any Twitter accounts.

**Did you, or do you, plan to make available an API that redistributes Twitter content to your customers, either as part of your product or as a complement? If so, please provide us with a sample payload.**

No. The API will only be used by me.

**In addition to the use case description, please disclose if your product, service, or analysis makes Twitter content or derived information available to a government entity (or entity who serves government entities).**

No. This will be used only for academic purpose and will be shared as public information via libraries and doesn't serve or provide service to any government entities.

1. **If yes, please provide a list of which government or public sector entities will have access to Twitter content, or information derived from Twitter content, under this use case:** N/A

2. **Also, we will need a description of which portion(s) of your overall use cases are applicable to each entity; or if they differ from the overall use case, a description of the specific use cases for these entities:** N/A

# Appendix B

## Twitter Customer Order Form

**Twitter Customer Order Form**

This Order Form ("Order") and Customer's use of the Services and Licensed Materials is subject to and governed by the Twitter Master License Agreement located at **https://legal.twitter.com/data-terms/us/mla.html**, including the Twitter Developer Policy located at **https://developer.twitter.com/en/developer-terms/policy**. Capitalized terms used in this Order will have the respective meanings ascribed to them in the Master License Agreement.

| **Customer** (or "you" as defined in Master License Agreement) | | **Bill to Party** | |
|---|---|---|---|
| | Purdue University | | Purdue University |
| Address | 100 N. University<br>West lafayette, IN<br>BRNG 2253<br>US | Address | 100 N. University<br>West lafayette,IN<br>BRNG 2253<br>US |
| | | Contact | Sweta Baniya<br>baniya@purdue.edu<br>5712089452 |

| **Order Information** | | | |
|---|---|---|---|
| Twitter Sales Contact | Emily Ashley | Twitter Account Manager | Kevin Dolezal |
| Order Effective Date | 12/10/2019 | Order Term | 12/10/2019 - 12/9/2020 |
| Customer PO | | | This Order will commence on the Order Effective Date and will remain effective for the Order Term (defined above), unless otherwise terminated earlier in accordance the Agreement. This Order is not effective until signed by both parties. |
| Adminerator Console Number -Account Name | 2258--Purdue | | |
| **Customer Application** | The core use of the case is for academic purposes only. Twitter APIs will only be used for academic research purposes. There are no profit-generating activities, but this academic research is a contribution to society.<br>Since this is a work without any profit of customers. There is no delivery to the customers. Twitter users will not be analyzed. Their identities will not be revealed in any case. If there is a chance that the identities of the Twitter users will be revealed then, all of them will be anonymized. My research has been approved by IRB at Purdue University. The research during the data collection as well as analysis will adhere to the IRB protocol that protects all the human subjects that are related with the research. For the analysis: I will be using "Social Network Analysis" via Nvivo to generate networks to see how people have networked via twitter. For this research, there will be no analysis of only the keywords but not the whole tweet.<br><br>The list of topic to be researched are:<br><br>1) Transnational Interaction<br>2) How do people network via Twitter during a disaster?<br><br>Here are my broader research questions:<br><br>1.How did transnational assemblage of official and unofficial communities formed in Nepal and Puerto Rico to mitigate the challenges of two different disasters?<br>2.What are the unique digital rhetorical and participatory actions of the assemblages in Nepal and Puerto Rico that helped in performing crisis communications transnationally?<br>3.What are the non-western, decolonized, and western practices of knowledge making during disaster that we can explore to compose and communicate better to help vulnerable populations in need?<br><br>The keywords will be used to analyze for example: how many people have used hashtag | | |

| | |
|---|---|
| | #NepalEarthquake or have used keywords like relief, rescue, help, donate. Only the numerical value will be analyzed. The content of the Tweets, as well as the identities displayers such as photographs or location or personal details, will not be used.<br>For the purpose of sharing, the results of Social Network Analysis will be presented in the form of written publication - the first will be my dissertation project, the second will be publications, and the third will be conferences. These are purely academic audiences and thus, there will be no profit-making involved in this.<br>As mentioned above, the exact content of the Tweets wouldn't be displayed. However, the content if necessary to be displayed will be done during classroom activities, conferences, and peer-reviewed academic publications. Again, the identity of Twitter accounts will not be disclosed. Any tweets that disclose personal details and information will not be used for the dissemination. This way, the information shared will be able to protect the identities of the people. The results of social network analysis are displayed in the form of maps and charts and graphs - hence, there will not be any information that is related to the human subjects (Twitter users) will be displayed. Only the numbers will be displayed. Additionally, the research doesn't involve Tweeting, Retweeting, or liking the content or interaction with any Twitter accounts.<br>The API will only be used by me. There will be no redistribution of Twitter content via a third-party API. Twitter content will not be made available to a government entity. This will be used only for **academic purpose and will be shared as public information via libraries and doesn't serve or** provides service to any government entities.<br><br>**User Protection and Government Use**. The provisions of Section 14.2 and Section 14.3 of the Agreement shall take precedent over any conflicting or inconsistent provisions set out in this Customer Application. |

**Services and Fees**

| Service | Price - Fees | Quantity | Unit of Measure | Start Date | End Date |
|---|---|---|---|---|---|
| Twitter Historical PowerTrack-Single Job | $2,500.00 | 1 | | 12/10/2019 | 12/9/2020 |

**Total One Time Charges:** $2,500.00

**Incorporated Terms.** As set out and incorporated in the Master License Agreement and Developer Policy, Customer may also be subject to the following terms where applicable: as it relates to your display of any of the Twitter Content, the Display Requirements located at **https://developer.twitter.com/en/developer-terms/display-requirements**; as it relates to your access to Twitter European Data, the Data Protection Addendum located at **https://gdpr.twitter.com/en/controller-to-controller-transfers.html**; as it relates to your use and display of the Twitter Marks, the Twitter Brand Assets and Guidelines located at **https://twitter.com/logo**; and as it relates to taking automated actions on your account, the Automation Rules located at **https://support.twitter.com/articles/76915** (**"Automation Rules"**).

**Additional Product Terms.** If you access or receive the Enterprise Data Collector, Engagement API, Account and Activity API, or InsightsTrack you agree to applicable terms located at **https://legal.twitter.com/data-terms/us/additional-terms.html**, which are hereby incorporated into the Agreement by reference.

| | |
|---|---|
| **Business/Pricing Terms:** | Nepal Earthquake:<br>Date Range: 4/24/2015-5/1/2015<br>Operators:<br>place: Nepal OR Asia OR Europe OR United States OR Australia OR Latin America (#NepalEarthquake OR #earthquake OR #QuakeNepal OR #quakeNepal OR #earthquakenepal OR #EarthquakeNepal OR #NepalEarthquakeRelief OR #NepalQuakeRelief OR #Pray4Nepal OR #prayfornepal OR #NepalQuake OR #NepalRelief OR #NepalRises)<br><br>Hurricane Maria:<br>Date Range: 9/17/2017 - 9/24/2017<br>Operators: (#Hurricane OR #HurricaneMaria OR #Relief OR #PuertoRico OR #Boricua OR #Relief OR #StayStrong OR #ReliefEfforts OR #Help OR #PuertoRicoStrong OR #PuertoRicoRelief OR #ClimateChange OR #UnitedForPuertoRico OR #PuertoRicoWillRise OR YoNoMe**Quito OR #EchaPa'Lante OR #SePuede OR #BastaYa OR #Pa'Arriba OR #VamosPa'Encima OR #PuertoRicoLoHaceMejor OR #HuracanMaria OR #UnidosPorPuertoRico** OR #PuertoRicoStrong OR #Comfort4PuertoRico OR #LatinaInfluencersCoalition OR #Maria) |

| |
|---|
| Customer agrees to not publish any analysis or results of analysis of Follower Graph data without written permission from Twitter. Prohibited publication types include marketing PDFs, blog posts, videos, or public speaking engagements. Customer may, however, market that Customer provides access to insights derived from the relevant endpoints and communicate how the Customer Service works to analyze this data. |
| Native geo data prior to 9/1/2011 is not available from Twitter; Language Detection, and URL Expansion enrichments prior to 3/26/2012 are not available; Profile Geo prior to 8/1/2013 are not available. All data prior to 1/1/2011 contains user profile information as it appeared in that user's profile in September 2011. |
| For historical products, Customer is charged based on the number of days and activities requested through Customer's given rules ("Job") and are determined based upon the calendar month in which the Jobs were completed. The smallest unit of time in which a Job can be completed is one (1) Historical Day. A Historical Day is any calendar day in UTC time that the historical job timeframe touches. For example if one asks for a historical job that went from 11:59pm to 12:01am, this would count as 2 historical days. |
| Upon completion of a historical job, the Twitter Content will only be available for download **for 15 calendar days**. If the Twitter Content is not downloaded by the 15th day, there may be additional charges to re-run the job. |
| *All rights to Twitter Content granted through the Agreement and this Order Form shall **terminate 12 months from the Order Effective Date**. |
| **Additional Payment Terms.** On the Effective Date, Twitter will invoice Customer for the fees indicated above, which will be due upon receipt. Payment must be accepted by Twitter prior to delivery of data. |
| **Receipt and Review of Terms and Exhibits.** Customer acknowledges that it has received and reviewed the Twitter Master License Agreement, the Twitter Developer Policy, the Incorporated Terms, the Additional Product Terms and other terms or exhibits incorporated into this Order. Customer understands and agrees the Twitter Master License Agreement, the Twitter Developer Policy, the Incorporated Terms, the Additional Product Terms and other terms or exhibits incorporated into this Order are part of this Order. |
| **Entire Agreement; Counterparts; Originals.** This document (including the Twitter Master License Agreement, the Twitter Developer Policy, the Incorporated Terms, the Additional Product Terms), and any applicable exhibits and applicable supplementary terms as defined herein constitutes the entire agreement of the parties and supersedes all prior communications, understandings and agreements relating to the subject matter hereof, whether oral or written. No term or condition contained in Customer's purchase order or similar document will apply unless agreed upon hereunder, even if Twitter has accepted the order set forth in such purchase order, and all such terms or conditions are otherwise hereby expressly rejected by Twitter. This Agreement may only be amended by a written document signed by authorized representatives of Twitter and Customer. This Order may be executed in two or more counterparts, each of which will be deemed an original, but all of which together shall constitute one and the same instrument. |

| **AGREED:** | | **ACCEPTED:** | |
|---|---|---|---|
| **Customer:** | Purdue University | **Twitter:** | Twitter International Company |
| **By:** | Sweta Baniya (Dec 10, 2019) | **By:** | Laurence O'Brien (Dec 11, 2019) |
| **Name** | Sweta Baniya | **Name** | Laurence O'Brien |
| **Title** | Graduate Student | **Title** | EMEA Controller |
| **Date** | Dec 10, 2019 | **Date** | Dec 11, 2019 |

# Appendix C

## Interview Questions

1. Where were you during the earthquake/hurricane?
2. Can you tell me what technology you used to contact your family or friends after the earthquake/hurricane?
3. After the earthquake/hurricane, who (organizations, government, volunteers, family members abroad, etc.) came to support you, and how long did it take you to get any help?
4. Have you been involved in working voluntarily in your community to do relief and rescue works on your own, or via any organization or network during or after the earthquake/hurricane?
5. If you were involved, could you tell me what you did exactly during the disaster to work, communicate, and support your community?
6. What methods of communication did you use to create connection in the community that you were serving?
7. Immediately after the earthquake/hurricane, how did you try to connect with other government officials, community members, media, health workers, or any other organizations?
8. How do you feel about the help you received and the support you provided to the community? Was it appropriate and effective?
9. In the long term, what groups or organizations have stayed connected with you, and which ones have fallen away?
10. Did you participate in any interpersonal networks during and after the disaster? For example: Facebook, Twitter, or any networks within or outside your community.

**VARIATIONS FOR THE OFFICIALS:**

1. How did your organization network with other organizations?
2. How did the affected people and their families communicate with you?
3. How did you reach out to the community/people who were affected?

4. Is your organization still part of the reconstruction efforts in these communities? What are the specific programs that you are launching?

---

# Appendix D

## Disaster and Crisis Communication Course Syllabus

### COURSE DESCRIPTION

**Disaster and Crisis Communication** is designed for English majors in the Professional Writing option. In this course, students will focus on how scientific, technical, and professional communication influence, and are influenced by, public discourse. Drawing on strategies of rhetorical criticism, students will gain an understanding of the persuasive value of style, arrangement, and delivery by investigating their professional roles in helping to structure public debate. Specifically, this course will focus on writing in and about addressing global issues such as climate change, disasters via risk and crisis communication. Communicating during a crisis has never been so important given the challenges of the current world. We will also explore practical strategies that any organization can develop to address situations of crisis that helps not only themselves but their community as well. In this course, we will interrogate:

- How can technical communicators contribute to disaster-related communications that are socially responsible?
- What does it mean to incorporate social justice in disaster-related communication?
- What are the current conversations that are ongoing regarding risk and crisis communication?
- What are the current public discourses surrounding disasters?

We will engage with these questions and learn to conduct a rhetorical analysis of various communications materials addressing the situation of a disaster. In addition, we will learn to conduct research, and design various products that could help in communicating crises. As with other Senior Seminars, the course will be reading and writing intensive, with a focus on abstract reasoning and deep engagement with theoretical texts.

### COURSE OBJECTIVES

With successful completion of this course, you will be able to:

- analyze the social, political, and cultural effects of professional and public discourse using principles of rhetorical criticism and concepts within risk and crisis communication;

- explain the interplay of rhetoric and ethics in formulating professional and public policies;
- draw logical connections across multiple texts, ideas, objects, and bodies;
- compose analyses in a variety of media about professional or public issues.

## COURSE MATERIALS AND REQUIREMENTS

- We will read excerpted journal articles or book chapters/essays available via our online course site.
- Students should expect to spend an average of 6 hours per week on this 3-credit course, outside of our regularly scheduled class meeting times.
- Note that any group work assigned in this class may also require you to meet with your group outside of class time.

## ASSIGNMENTS AND GRADING

Below are the major assignments for the class.

### Weekly Reading Response: 300 Points

You will have a total of **ten weekly responses** starting Week 2. You will be expected to write a 500-word reading response in which you will do the following: (a) synthesize, summarize, and analyze the readings assigned for the week and (b) connect these readings to the issue or the topic that you want to explore in this course.

### Discussion Facilitation: 100 Points

For one class session, you will be responsible for facilitating discussion about that day's reading assignment. The goal is to help us come to an understanding of what the reading was about, key concepts and ideas from the readings, and how the reading connects to other readings, ideas, and discussions.

### Assignment #1: Rhetorical Analysis & Editing Wiki: 300 Points

1. **Editing Wikipedia:** In this assignment, based on your readings and research about a particular crisis, you will make edits to a Wikipedia page. These edits can be minor copyedit, adding references, check facts. This includes participating in edit-a-thon.

2. **Rhetorical Analysis of a Crisis:** In this assignment, you will conduct a rhetorical analysis of a particular crisis and the situation of the crisis. In your analysis I want you to think about what kinds of communication strategies were used to address this crisis both formally and informally.

### Assignment #2: Final Seminar Project: 300 Points

For our final semester project, you will work in groups to conduct narrative inquiry and develop a communications strategy and a backgrounder on the crisis and immediate response. This will be followed by a digital exhibition.

## SCHEDULE WITH READING LIST

This course is divided into various three themes. At the very beginning of the course, there is an introduction to various terms and terminologies. With the second theme, the students will learn about disaster and crisis specific research within rhetoric, technical communication, and beyond. The final theme is crisis and technology which focusses on uses of digital technologies in disaster response and research within those. Instructors can refine the readings based on the class requirements and change the assignment sequences. This course can be taught as an undergraduate/graduate level course. Moreover, there is workshop element to this course where students will engage learning about qualitative data collection and analysis methods within class time. Hence, instructors can modify those specific details as needed.

### Theme #1: Introduction to Disaster, Crisis Communication Terminologies

Theme #1 will focus on introduction of key terms that are relevant to disaster and crisis communication and will focus on learning how to edit Wikipedia and how to conduct a rhetorical analysis of a disaster related communication.

#### *Week One: Introduction*

1. Introduction to the Course, Syllabus
2. Twigg, John. *Disaster Risk Reduction.* Chapter 1
3. ISDR Terminology on Disaster Risk Reduction
4. Kelman, Ilan. "Lost for Words Amongst Disaster Risk Science Vocabulary?" *International Journal of Disaster Risk Science*, vol. 9, no. 3, Sept. 2018, pp. 281–91. *Springer Link*, https://doi.org/10.1007/s13753-018-0188-3.

⇒ *Introduce Unit #1*

***Week Two: Types of Risk, Disasters & Intro to Crisis Communication***

1. Ritchie, Liesel, and Duane Gill. "Considering COVID-19 through the Lens of Hazard and Disaster Research." *Social Sciences*, vol. 10, no. 7, 7, July 2021, p. 248. https://www.mdpi.com, https://doi.org/10.3390/socsci10070248.
2. Coombs, W. Timothy. "Conceptualizing Crisis Communication." *Handbook of Risk and Crisis Communication*, edited by Robert L. Heath, and H. Dan O'Hair, Taylor & Francis Group, 2008, pp. 99-118
3. Strother, J. B. "Crisis Communication Put to the Test: The Case of Two Airlines on 9/11." *IEEE Transactions on Professional Communication*, vol. 47, no. 4, Dec. 2004, pp. 290–300. *IEEE Xplore*, https://doi.org/10.1109/TPC.2004.837981.

⇒ *Preparation for Wikipedia Workshop*

***Week Three: Wikipedia Workshop & Understanding Risk /Crisis Comm***

1. Schwarz, Andreas, et al. "Significance and Structure of International Risk and Crisis Communication Research." *The Handbook of International Crisis Communication Research*, John Wiley & Sons, Ltd, 2016, pp. 1–10. *Wiley Online Library*, https://doi.org/10.1002/9781118516812.ch1.
2. Horsley, J. Suzanne, and Randolph T. Barker. "Toward a Synthesis Model for Crisis Communication in the Public Sector: An Initial Investigation." *Journal of Business and Technical Communication*, vol. 16, no. 4, Oct. 2002, pp. 406–40. *Crossref*, https://doi.org/10.1177/105065102236525.
3. Knight, Melinda. "Managing Risk and Crisis Communication." *Business and Professional Communication Quarterly*, vol. 77, no. 4, Dec. 2014, pp. 355–56. *SAGE Journals*, https://doi.org/10.1177/2329490614561021.

***Week Four: Wiki Edi-a-Thon & Work Week***

1. Organize a Wikipedia Editing Workshop and Edit-a-Thon. (Note: This can be organized via CCCCs Wikipedia Initiative Members or via libraries at the institution)

⇒ *Assignment I Part I Wiki editing report Due*

### Theme #2 Disasters and Humanitarian Crisis Research

Theme #2 will focus on Disasters and Humanitarian Crisis Research in which students will learn about various research that technical communication and communication scholars have done that includes primary and secondary research including the grassroots movement. Teachers will also introduce Assignment #2 that is focused on research, developing communication strategy, and creating a website.

#### *Week Five: Rhetoric of Risk and Technical Communication*

1. Reamer, David. "'Risk = Probability × Consequences': Probability, Uncertainty, and the Nuclear Regulatory Commission's Evolving Risk Communication Rhetoric." *Technical Communication Quarterly*, vol. 24, no. 4, Oct. 2015, pp. 349–73. *Taylor and Francis+NEJM*, https://doi.org/10.1080/10572252.2015.1079334.
2. Ding, Huiling. "Transcultural Risk Communication and Viral Discourses: Grassroots Movements to Manage Global Risks of H1N1 Flu Pandemic." *Technical Communication Quarterly*, vol. 22, no. 2, 2013, pp. 126–49. *purdue-primo-prod.com*, https://doi.org/10.1080/10572252.2013.746628.

⇒ *Introduce Assignment #2*

#### *Week Six: Disaster and Public Reactions*

1. Coombs, W. Timothy, and Sherry Jean Holladay. "How Publics React to Crisis Communication Efforts: Comparing Crisis Response Reactions across Sub-Arenas." *Journal of Communication Management*; London, vol. 18, no. 1, 2014, pp. 40–57. *ProQuest*, https://doi.org/10.1108/JCOM-03-2013-0015.
2. Yum, Jung-Yoon, and Se-Hoon Jeong. "Examining the Public's Responses to Crisis Communication From the Perspective of Three Models of Attribution." *Journal of Business and Technical Communication*, vol. 29, no. 2, Apr. 2015, pp. 159–83. *SAGE Journals*, https://doi.org/10.1177/1050651914560570.
3. Yan Jin. "Making Sense Sensibly in Crisis Communication: How Publics' Crisis Appraisals Influence Their Negative Emotions, Coping Strategy Preferences, and Crisis Response Acceptance." *Communication Research*, vol. 37, no. 4, Aug. 2010, pp. 522–52. *Crossref*, https://doi.org/10.1177/0093650210368256.

⇒ *Conduct workshop on methodologies for Rhetorical Analysis*

### *Week Seven: Disaster and Global Grassroots Movement*

1. Jahanian, Mohammad, et al. "DiReCT: Disaster Response Coordination with Trusted Volunteers." 2019 International Conference on Information and Communication Technologies for Disaster Management (ICT-DM), 2019, pp. 1–8. *IEEE Xplore*, https://doi.org/10.1109/ICT-DM47966.2019.9032915.
2. Baniya, Sweta. "Transnational Assemblages in Disaster Response: Networked Communities, Technologies, and Coalitional Actions During Global Disasters." *Technical Communication Quarterly*, vol. 31, no. 4, Oct. 2022, pp. 326–42. *Taylor and Francis+NEJM*, https://doi.org/10.1080/10572252.2022.2034973.
3. Soto Vega, Karrieann. "Puerto Rico Weathers the Storm: Autogestión as a Coalitional Counter-Praxis of Survival." *Feral Feminisms*, no. 9, 2019, p. 17.

### *Week Eight: Workshop & Work Week*

Conduct a writing workshop rhetorical analysis for one class period. The second-class period can be given as a work day. Workdays are designed for students to have a dedicated time to work on their project.

- Conduct a writing workshop on Rhetorical Analysis
- *Assignment #1 Part-II: Rhetorical Analysis Due*

## Theme #3 Crisis and Technology

Theme #3 will focus on research and publications related to Crisis and Technology. Varieties of articles curated within this theme discusses disaster response and uses of technologies by various communities across the world. Students also will learn to write conduct research.

### *Week Nine: Social Media and Disaster*

1. Potts, Liza. *Social Media in Disaster Response: How Experience Architects Can Build for Participation*. Routledge, 2014. Chapter 1
2. Murthy, Dhiraj, and Alexander J. Gross. "Social Media Processes in Disasters: Implications of Emergent Technology Use." *Social Science Research*, vol. 63, Mar. 2017, pp. 356–70. *ScienceDirect*, https://doi.org/10.1016/j.ssresearch.2016.09.015.
3. Cho, Seong Eun, et al. "Social Media Use during Japan's 2011 Earthquake: How Twitter Transforms the Locus of Crisis Communication." *Media International Australia*, vol.

149, no. 1, Nov. 2013, pp. 28–40. *Crossref*, https://doi.org/10.1177/1329878X1314900105.

⇒ *Introduce Qualitative Research Strategies, Data Collection*

### *Week Ten: Feminist Response to Disaster*

1. Mwebaza, Rose. "Gender, Climate Change and Disaster Risk Reduction." UNDP Presentation.
2. Resurrección, Bernadette P. "Persistent Women and Environment Linkages in Climate Change and Sustainable Development Agendas." *Women's Studies International Forum*, vol. 40, Sept. 2013, pp. 33–43. *ScienceDirect*, https://doi.org/10.1016/j.wsif.2013.03.011.
3. Baniya, Sweta. "Managing Environmental Risks in the Age of Climate Change: Rhetorical Agency and Ecological Literacies of Transnational Women During the April 2015 Nepal Earthquake | Enculturation." *Enculturation*, 2020, http://enculturation.net/managing_environmental.

⇒ *Organize a writing workshop for research paper.*

### *Week Eleven: Designing a Digital Exhibition*

*Note to Teachers: Organize workshop on Designing Website for Exhibition. Teachers can partner with libraries at their institutions to organize this workshop.*

⇒ *Assignment # 2: Part I: Research Paper Due*

### *Week Twelve: Public Health Crisis and Misinformation*

1. Angeli, Elizabeth L., and Christina D. Norwood. "Responding to Public Health Crises: Bridging Collective Mindfulness and User Experience to Create Communication Interventions." *Communication Design Quarterly Review*, vol. 5, no. 2, 2017, pp. 29–39.
2. St.Amant, Kirk. "Communicating About COVID-19: Practices for Today, Planning for Tomorrow." *Journal of Technical Writing and Communication*, vol. 50, no. 3, July 2020, pp. 211–23. *SAGE Journals*, https://doi.org/10.1177/0047281620923589.
3. Tran, Thi, et al. "Misinformation Harms: A Tale of Two Humanitarian Crises." *IEEE Transactions on Professional Communication*, vol. 63, no. 4, Dec. 2020, pp. 386–99. *IEEE Xplore*, https://doi.org/10.1109/TPC.2020.3029685.

### *Week Thirteen: Effective Crisis Communication Strategies*

1. Baniya, Sweta, and Chen Chen. "Experiencing a Global Pandemic: The Power of Public Storytelling as Antenarrative in Crisis Communication." *Technical Communication*, vol. 68, no. 4, Nov. 2021, pp. 74–87.
2. Ngai, Cindy S. B., and Yan Jin. "The Effectiveness of Crisis Communication Strategies on Sina Weibo in Relation to Chinese Publics' Acceptance of These Strategies." *Journal of Business and Technical Communication*, vol. 30, no. 4, Oct. 2016, pp. 451–94. *SAGE Journals*, https://doi.org/10.1177/1050651916651907.
3. Lee, Betty Kaman. "Audience-Oriented Approach to Crisis Communication:: A Study of Hong Kong Consumers' Evaluation of an Organizational Crisis." *Communication Research*, vol. 31, no. 5, Oct. 2004, pp. 600–18. *SAGE Journals*, https://doi.org/10.1177/0093650204267936.

### *Week Fourteen: Students Meet To discuss the Website & Communication Strategy Plans*

*Students will meet to discuss their projects on Communications Strategy and the website design.*

### *Week Fifteen: Presentations*

### *Week Sixteen: Final Seminar Project Due*

# Appendix E

## Crisis Communication Assignment

This is the second and final assignment for your class. In this project, you will work in teams of two to a) conduct research, b) create a communications strategy with specific recommendations on handling a crisis, and c) present the results of this research and strategies publicly in the form of an exhibition and a presentation.

**Research: Conducting Narrative Inquiry and Analyzing a Crisis Response: 100 Points**

**Draft Due:**

**Revised Draft Based on Student Choice:**

With your previous experience of research in Assignment #1, in this assignment I want you to conduct collaborative research with narrative inquiry. Each group should choose from the following themes:

- Local (Virginia /East Coast)
- Regional (US OR Five US Territories)
- International (Beyond US—preferably Asia)

After choosing the theme, you should think about the following:

1. **Find a crisis:** What is the current event or crisis that interests you and your partner? Find a crisis that was not handled well OR handled well by an organization—government / non-governmental agencies OR grassroots people /agencies.
2. **Research how your chosen organization** has responded to this selected crisis. You can look for the following:
   a. documentation, reports, videos, press conferences
   b. posts (on Facebook, Twitter, Instagram, etc.)
   c. conversations with stakeholders (such as major interactions with customers or community members)
   d. media interactions (announcements, press releases, media coverage, sharing of news stories, etc.)
   e. other key messages and elements of the company or organization's handling of the crisis.

3. **Conduct a qualitative analysis** or narrative inquiry of the effectiveness of their crisis communication strategies: *What worked and what didn't?*
4. **Use theories** discussed in the class to analyze communications strategies.
5. **Provide Recommendation:** Provide at least two recommendations for improving their communications strategy: for example*: how can they make crisis communication people centered and why is that necessary?*
6. **Citation:** Cite the readings that we have read, cite articles and other researchers. This assignment is asking you to put whatever you have learned in this class into practice.
7. **Submission:**
   a. The paper should be at least **12 double spaces.**
   b. Should have an introduction, literature review section, methods, results, and recommendation sections.
   c. Should be in the Times New Roman/ 11 font & APA citation format
   d. Should display qualitative coding and pictures /images are optional

8. **Grading:**
   a. The papers will be graded on the quality of the data analysis, argument, and following the guidelines.

9. **Crisis Communication Strategy: 100 points**

In this part of the assignment, you are tasked with developing a crisis communication plan for local, regional, and international crises. This assignment asks you to develop practical strategies for handling a local, regional, and international crisis. You will be publicly exhibiting this assignment such that you contribute to the open knowledge. Please follow the directions below:

- explain the background of the crisis and provide a risk assessment process for this crisis
- outline challenges and opportunities that could come for crisis prevention, planning, response, and recovery
- this plan should include strategies for pre-crisis, crisis, and post-crisis
- include plans for social media and public messaging during a crisis and list any resources.
- **Submission:**

a. This plan should include all the listed items.
b. This document should be well designed (you can use canva.com)
c. This plan should be presented in a way that can be modifiable by any organization that wants to use it.

10. **Grading:**
    a. The grading for the Crisis Communication Strategy depends on the effectiveness of the crisis communication plan, design, and the adaptability of the plan and messaging.

11. **Web Exhibition, Presentation & Reflection (100 Points)**

The last part of this assignment requires you to curate your research and communications plan into a website. In this curation of your research, you will take help and support from me. For this part of the assignment, you are required to:

- **Artistic Presentation (50 points):** This part of the assignment asks you to present your research as well as your communication plan to the public using artistic ways: in its simplest form it can be a webpage where you curate your research, or you can choose creative ways to complete this task; for example, we can create a booklet of our strategies.
- **Presentation (25 points):** You and your group members will provide a 20-25-minute-long presentation to possibly a larger audience.
- **Reflection (25 points):** Final part of the assignment is curating a video reflection (3-4 minutes long) that can be used in your exhibition and including closed captions.
- **Grading:**
    a. The exhibition's grading will be based on professional curation of the information and webpage.
    b. Presentation's grading will be based on professional presentations, slideshow, and effective delivery.
    c. Reflection's grading will be based on fulfilling the criteria and submission

## Works Cited


Adsanatham, Chanon. "REDRES[ING] RHETORICA: A Methodological Proposal for Queering Cross-Cultural Rhetorical Studies." *Re/Orienting Writing Studies: Queer Methods, Queer Projects*, edited by William P. Banks et al., Utah State UP, 2019, pp. 75–94. *JSTOR*, http://www.jstor.org/stable/j.ctvdmx0hm.9.

Agboka, Godwin Y. "Decolonial Methodologies: Social Justice Perspectives in Intercultural Technical Communication Research." *Journal of Technical Writing and Communication*, vol. 44, no. 3, July 2014, pp. 297–327. *SAGE Journals*, https://doi.org/10.2190/TW.44.3.e.

Akena, Francis Adyanga. "Critical Analysis of the Production of Western Knowledge and Its Implications for Indigenous Knowledge and Decolonization." *Journal of Black Studies*, vol. 43, no. 6, 2012, pp. 599–619. *JSTOR*, https://www.jstor.org/stable/23414661.

Albala-Bertrand, J. M. "Natural Disaster Situations and Growth: A Macroeconomic Model for Sudden Disaster Impacts." *World Development*, vol. 21, no. 9, Sept. 1993, pp. 1417–34. *Crossref*, https://doi.org/10.1016/0305-750X(93)90122-P.

Aldrich, Daniel P. *Building Resilience: Social Capital in Post-Disaster Recovery*. The U of Chicago P, 2012.

Aldrich, Daniel P., et al., editors. *Resilience and Recovery in Asian Disasters: Community Ties, Market Mechanisms, and Governance*. Springer, 2015.

Angeli, Elizabeth L. *Rhetorical Work in Emergency Medical Services*. Routledge, 2018.

Appadurai, Arjun. *The Future as Cultural Fact: Essays on the Global Condition*. Verso, 2013.

Arola, Kristin L., and Adam C. Arola. "An Ethics of Assemblage: Creative Repetition and the Electric Pow Wow." *Assembling Composition*, edited by Kathleen Blake Yancey and Stephen J. McElroy, National Council of Teachers of English, 2017, pp. 204–21.

Baniya, Sweta. "The Implications of Transnational Coalitional Actions and Activism in Disaster Response." *Spark: A 4C4Equality Journal*, 23 Apr. 2021, https://sparkactivism.com/volume-3-call/transnational-coalitional-actions-and-activism-in-disaster-response/.

---. "Transnational Assemblages in Disaster Response: Networked Communities, Technologies, and Coalitional Actions During Global Disasters." *Technical Communication Quarterly*, vol. 31, no. 4, Jan. 2022, pp.

326-342. *Crossref*, https://doi.org/10.1080/10572252.2022.2034973.

---. "How Can Technical Communicators Help in Disaster Response?" *Technical Communication*, vol. 69, no. 2, May 2022, pp. 58–74. *Crossref*, https://doi.org/10.55177/tc658475.

Baniya, Sweta, et al. *Representing Diversity in Digital Research: Digital Feminist Ethics and Resisting Dominant Normatives*. 2018, p. 11.

Baniya, Sweta, and Liza Potts. "Experts, Knowledge Making, and Disaster Across Twitter." *The 40th ACM International Conference on Design of Communication*, ACM, 2022, pp. 9–14. *Crossref*, https://doi.org/10.1145/3513130.3558972.

Baniya, Sweta, and Chen Chen. "Experiencing a Global Pandemic: The Power of Public Storytelling as Antenarrative in Crisis Communication." *Technical Communication*, vol. 68, no. 4, Nov. 2021, pp. 74–87.

Barad, Karen Michelle. *Meeting the Universe Halfway: Quantum Physics and the Entanglement of Matter and Meaning*. Duke UP, 2007.

---. "Posthumanist Performativity: Toward an Understanding of How Matter Comes to Matter." *Signs*, vol. 28, no. 3, 2003, pp. 801–31. *JSTOR*, https://doi.org/10.1086/345321.

Belfi, E., and Nedra Sandiford. "What is decolonization, why is it important, and how can we practice it?" Interdependence: Global Solidarity and Local Actions. Decolonization Series Part 1: Exploring Decolonization. In S. Brandauer and E. Hartman (Eds.). *Interdependence: Global Solidarity and Local Actions.* The Community-based Global Learning Collaborative, 2021. https://www.cbglcollab.org/what-is-decolonization-why-is-it-important

Bennett, Jane. "The Force of Things: Steps toward an Ecology of Matter." *Political Theory*, vol. 32, no. 3, 2004, pp. 347–72. *JSTOR*, http://www.jstor.org/stable/4148158.

Bernard-Donals, Michael. "The Rhetoric of Disaster and the Imperative of Writing." *Rhetoric Society Quarterly*, vol. 31, no. 1, 2001, pp. 73–94. *JSTOR*, http://www.jstor.org/stable/3886402.

Boiarsky, Carolyn R. *Risk Communication and Miscommunication: Case Studies in Science, Technology, Engineering, Government and Community Organizations*. Utah State UP, 2016.

Bonilla, Yarimar. "The Coloniality of Disaster: Race, Empire, and the Temporal Logics of Emergency in Puerto Rico, USA." *Political Geography*, vol. 78, Apr. 2020, p. 102181. *Crossref*, https://doi.org/10.1016/j.polgeo.2020.102181.

Borgatti, Stephen P. *Analyzing Social Networks*. Sage, 2013.

Borgatti, Stephen P., and Martin G. Everett. "Network Analysis of 2-Mode Data." *Social Networks*, vol. 19, no. 3, Aug. 1997, pp. 243–69. *Crossref*, https://doi.org/10.1016/S0378-8733(96)00301-2.

Buchanan, Ian. "Assemblage Theory and Its Discontents." *Deleuze Stud-*

*ies*, vol. 9, no. 3, 2015, pp. 382–92. *JSTOR*, http://www.jstor.org/stable/45331821.

Castells, Manuel. "The New Public Sphere: Global Civil Society, Communication Networks, and Global Governance." *The ANNALS of the American Academy of Political and Social Science*, vol. 616, no. 1, Mar. 2008, pp. 78–93. *SAGE Journals*, https://doi.org/10.1177/0002716207311877.

Cedillo, Christina V. "Disabled and Undocumented: In/Visibility at the Borders of Presence, Disclosure, and Nation." *Rhetoric Society Quarterly*, vol. 50, no. 3, May 2020, pp. 203–11. *Crossref*, https://doi.org/10.1080/02773945.2020.1752131.

Chandran, Rina. "Nepal Quake Survivors Struggle with Debt, Raising Trafficking Fears." *Reuters*, 26 July 2016, https://www.reuters.com/article/us-nepal-quake-trafficking/nepal-quake-survivors-struggle-with-debt-raising-trafficking-fears-idUSKCN1061RJ.

Chávez, Karma R. "Counter-Public Enclaves and Understanding the Function of Rhetoric in Social Movement Coalition-Building." *Communication Quarterly*, vol. 59, no. 1, Jan. 2011, pp. 1–18. *Crossref*, https://doi.org/10.1080/01463373.2010.541333.

Cho, Seong Eun, et al. "Social Media Use during Japan's 2011 Earthquake: How Twitter Transforms the Locus of Crisis Communication." *Media International Australia*, vol. 149, no. 1, Nov. 2013, pp. 28–40. *Crossref*, https://doi.org/10.1177/1329878X1314900105.

Clandinin, D. Jean. *Engaging in Narrative Inquiry*. Routledge, Taylor & Francis Group, 2016.

Clark, Erin. *Feminist Technical Communication Apparent Feminisms, Slow Crisis, and the Deepwater Horizon Disaster*. Utah State UP, 2023.

"Climate Risk Profile: Nepal." *Climatelinks*, 19 July 2017, https://www.climatelinks.org/resources/climate-risk-profile-nepal.

Collins, Patricia Hill. *Intersectionality As Critical Social Theory*. Duke UP, 2019.

Connors, Robert J. "Rise of Technical Writing Instruction in America." *Journal of Technical Writing and Communication*, vol. 12, no. 4, 1982, pp. 329–52. https://doi.org/10.1177/004728168201200406.

Coombs, W. Timothy. "Protecting Organization Reputations During a Crisis: The Development and Application of Situational Crisis Communication Theory." *Corporate Reputation Review*, vol. 10, no. 3, Sept. 2007, pp. 163–76. *Crossref*, https://doi.org/10.1057/palgrave.crr.1550049.

Coombs, W. Timothy, and Sherry Jean Holladay. "How Publics React to Crisis Communication Efforts: Comparing Crisis Response Reactions across Sub-Arenas." *Journal of Communication Management; London*, vol. 18, no. 1, 2014, pp. 40–57. *ProQuest*, https://doi.org/10.1108/

JCOM-03-2013-0015.

Cooper, Marilyn M. "Rhetorical Agency as Emergent and Enacted." *College Composition and Communication*, vol. 62, no. 3, 2011, pp. 420–49. *JSTOR*, http://www.jstor.org/stable/27917907.

Cortés, Jason. "Puerto Rico: Hurricane Maria and the Promise of Disposability." *Capitalism Nature Socialism*, vol. 29, no. 3, July 2018, pp. 1–8. https://doi.org/10.1080/10455752.2018.1505233.

Crenshaw, Kimberlé Williams. "Intersectionality, Identity Politics and Violence Against Women of Color." Kvinder, Køn & Forskning, no. 2–3, June 2006. *Crossref*, https://doi.org/10.7146/kkf.v0i2-3.28090.

Crooks, Andrew, et al. "#Earthquake: Twitter as a Distributed Sensor System." *Transactions in GIS*, vol. 17, no. 1, 2013, pp. 124–47. https://doi.org/10.1111/j.1467-9671.2012.01359.x.

Dadas, Caroline. "Chapter 1. Hashtag Activism: The Promise and Risk of 'Attention.'" *Social Writing/Social Media: Publics, Presentations, and Pedagogies*, edited by Douglas M. Walls and Stephanie Vie, The WAC Clearinghouse / UP of Colorado, 2017, pp. 17–36. *Crossref*, https://doi.org/10.37514/PER-B.2017.0063.2.01.

DeLanda, Manuel. *Assemblage Theory*. Edinburgh UP, 2016.

Deleuze, Gilles, and Félix Guattari. *A Thousand Plateaus: Capitalism and Schizophrenia*. Translated by Brian Massumi, U of Minnesota P, 1987.

Delgado, Teresa. *A Puerto Rican Decolonial Theology: Prophesy Freedom*. Springer International Publishing AG, 2017.

Ding, Huiling. *Rhetoric of a Global Epidemic: Transcultural Communication about SARS*. Southern Illinois UP, 2014.

---. "Social Media and Participatory Risk Communication During the H1n1 Flu Epidemic: A Comparative Study of the United States and China.(Report)." *China Media Report Overseas*, vol. 6, no. 4, 2010, p. 80.

Dingo, Rebecca. *Networking Arguments: Rhetoric, Transnational Feminism, and Public Policy Writing*. U of Pittsburgh P, 2012.

Disaster | United Nations Office of Disaster Risk Reduction. 30 Aug. 2007, http://www.undrr.org/terminology/disaster.

"Disaster Activation: Nepal Earthquake 2015." *Humanitarian OpenStreetMap Team*, 27 Apr. 2015, https://www.hotosm.org/projects/nepal_2015_earthquake_response.

Edbauer, Jenny. "Unframing Models of Public Distribution: From Rhetorical Situation to Rhetorical Ecologies." *Rhetoric Society Quarterly*, vol. 35, no. 4, Sept. 2005, pp. 5–24. *Crossref*, https://doi.org/10.1080/02773940509391320.

Edwards, Dustin, and Heather Lang. "Entanglements That Matter": A New Materialist Trace of #YesAllWomen." *Circulation, Writing, and Rhetoric*, edited by Laurie E. Gries and Collin Gifford Brooke, Utah State UP, 2018, pp. 118–34. *JSTOR*, https://doi.org/10.2307/j.ctt21668mb.10.

Ehrenfeld, Dan. "'Sharing a World with Others': Rhetoric's Ecological Turn and the Transformation of the Networked Public Sphere." *Rhetoric Society Quarterly*, vol. 50, no. 5, Oct. 2020, pp. 305–20. *Crossref*, https://doi.org/10.1080/02773945.2020.1813321.

Feliú-Mójer, Mónica. "I Won't Leave Puerto Rico In The Dark." *Medium*, 18 July 2019, https://brightthemag.com/puerto-rico-hurricane-activism-health-e58ac1884f96.

Frandsen, Finn, and Winni Johansen. "Crisis Communication, Complexity, and the Cartoon Affair: A Case Study." *The Handbook of Crisis Communication*, edited by W. Timothy Coombs and Sherry J. Holladay, John Wiley & Sons, Ltd, 2010, pp. 425–48. https://doi.org/10.1002/9781444314885.ch21.

Frith, Jordan. "Social Network Analysis and Professional Practice: Exploring New Methods for Researching Technical Communication." *Technical Communication Quarterly*, vol. 23, no. 4, Oct. 2014, pp. 288–302. *Crossref*, https://doi.org/10.1080/10572252.2014.942467.

Frost, Erin A. "Transcultural Risk Communication on Dauphin Island: An Analysis of Ironically Located Responses to the Deepwater Horizon Disaster." *Technical Communication Quarterly*, vol. 22, no. 1, Jan. 2013, pp. 50–66. *Taylor and Francis+NEJM*, https://doi.org/10.1080/10572252.2013.726483.

Garcia, Ivis. "The Lack of Proof of Ownership in Puerto Rico Is Crippling Repairs in the Aftermath of Hurricane Maria." *Human Rights*, vol. 44, no. 2, 2019, pp. 20–23.

Garrett, Mary. "Tied to a Tree: Culture and Self-Reflexivity." *Rhetoric Society Quarterly*, vol. 43, no. 3, May 2013, pp. 243–55. *Crossref*, https://doi.org/10.1080/02773945.2013.792693.

Geisler, Cheryl. "How Ought We to Understand the Concept of Rhetorical Agency? Report from the ARS." *Rhetoric Society Quarterly*, vol. 34, no. 3, June 2004, pp. 9–17. *Crossref*, https://doi.org/10.1080/02773940409391286.

Goswami, Rupak, et al. *Social Network Analysis in the Context of Community Response to Disaster*. SAGE Publications Ltd, 2018. *Crossref*, https://doi.org/10.4135/9781526444622.

Government of Nepal. Nepal Earthquake 2015 Post Disaster Needs Assessment Vol. A: Key Findings. Government of Nepal, National Planning Commission, 2015.

Grabill, Jeffrey T., and W. Michele Simmons. "Toward a Critical Rhetoric of Risk Communication: Producing Citizens and the Role of Technical Communicators." *Technical Communication Quarterly*, vol. 7, no. 4, Sept. 1998, pp. 415–41. *Crossref*, https://doi.org/10.1080/10572259809364640.

Grace, Rob, and Jason Chew Kit Tham. "Adapting Uncertainty Reduction Theory for Crisis Communication: Guidelines for Technical Communicators." *Journal of Business and Technical Communication*, vol. 35, no. 1, Jan. 2021, pp. 110–17. *SAGE Journals*, https://doi.org/10.1177/1050651920959188.

Haas, Angela M. "Race, Rhetoric, and Technology: A Case Study of Decolonial Technical Communication Theory, Methodology, and Pedagogy." *Journal of Business and Technical Communication*, vol. 26, no. 3, July 2012, pp. 277–310. *Crossref*, https://doi.org/10.1177/1050651912439539.

Haas, Angela M., and Michelle F. Eble. "Introduction: THE SOCIAL JUSTICE TURN." *Key Theoretical Frameworks: Teaching Technical Communication in the Twenty-First Century*, edited by Angela M. Haas and Michelle F. Eble, Utah State UP, 2018, pp. 3–20.

Haff, P. K. "Technology as a Geological Phenomenon: Implications for Human Well-Being." *Geological Society, London, Special Publications*, vol. 395, no. 1, 2014, pp. 301–09. *Crossref*, https://doi.org/10.1144/SP395.4.

Hall, M. L., et al. "The 2015 Nepal Earthquake Disaster: Lessons Learned One Year On." *Public Health*, vol. 145, Apr. 2017, pp. 39–44. *ScienceDirect*, https://doi.org/10.1016/j.puhe.2016.12.031.

Harlan, Castle. Update: Burger King's Recovery in Puerto Rico from Hurricane Maria. https://www.prnewswire.com/news-releases/update--burger-kings-recovery-in-puerto-rico-from-hurricane-maria-300533216.html. Accessed 21 Mar. 2024.

Hawhee, Debra. *A Sense of Urgency: How the Climate Crisis Is Changing Rhetoric*. U of Chicago P, 2023.

Hayles, N. Katherine. *How We Became Posthuman Virtual Bodies in Cybernetics, Literature, and Informatics*. U of Chicago P, 1999.

Hesford, Wendy S., and Eileen E. Schell. "Introduction: Configurations of Transnationality: Locating Feminist Rhetorics." *College English,* vol. 70, no. 5, May 2008, pp. 461–70. *ProQuest*, http://search.proquest.com/docview/236932658/citation/50013FBD68D245BBPQ/1.

Hinojosa, Jennifer, and Edwin Meléndez. *Puerto Rican Exodus: One Year Since Hurricane Maria*. Research Brief. Centro: Center for Puerto Rican Studies. Issued September 2018.

Hinojosa, Jennifer, and Edwin Meléndez. *The Housing Crisis in Puerto Rico and the Impact of Hurricane Maria**. Centro: Center for Puerto Rican Studies. Issued June 2018.

Horsley, J. Suzanne, and Randolph T. Barker. "Toward a Synthesis Model for Crisis Communication in the Public Sector: An Initial Investigation." *Journal of Business and Technical Communication*, vol. 16, no. 4, Oct. 2002, pp. 406–40. *Crossref*, https://doi.org/10.1177/105065102236525.

Itchuaqiyaq, Cana Uluak, and Breeanne Matheson. "Decolonizing Decoloniality: Considering the (Mis)Use of Decolonial Frameworks in TPC Scholarship." *Communication Design Quarterly*, vol. 9, no. 1, May 2021, pp. 20–31, https://doi.org/10.1145/3437000.3437002.

Jha, Kalpana. "Women's Representation and Intersectional (Un)Inclusion." *The Record*, 17 Mar. 2022, https://www.recordnepal.com/womens-representation-and-intersectional-uninclusion?fbclid=IwAR3I2yL3bwV4T9pcN3Pxg8usy0Vhuvj-f9tsnJpK9rPehWXa-p49mN9s4yws.

Jones, Madison. "A Counterhistory of Rhetorical Ecologies." *Rhetoric Society Quarterly*, vol. 51, no. 4, Aug. 2021, pp. 336–52. *Crossref*, https://doi.org/10.1080/02773945.2021.1947517.

Jones, Natasha N. "Rhetorical Narratives of Black Entrepreneurs: The Business of Race, Agency, and Cultural Empowerment." *Journal of Business and Technical Communication*, vol. 31, no. 3, July 2017, pp. 319–49. *Crossref*, https://doi.org/10.1177/1050651917695540.

---. "Narrative Inquiry in Human-Centered Design: Examining Silence and Voice to Promote Social Justice in Design Scenarios." *Journal of Technical Writing and Communication*, vol. 46, no. 4, Oct. 2016, pp. 471–92. *Crossref*, https://doi.org/10.1177/0047281616653489.

Jones, Natasha N., et al. "Disrupting the Past to Disrupt the Future: An Antenarrative of Technical Communication." *Technical Communication Quarterly*, vol. 25, no. 4, 2016, pp. 211–29. *purdue-primo-prod.com*, https://doi.org/10.1080/10572252.2016.1224655.

Kharpal, A (2017, Oct). Mark Zuckerberg apologizes after critics slam his 'magical' virtual reality tour of Puerto Rico devastation. CNBC. https://www.cnbc.com/2017/10/10/facebook-ceo-mark-zuckerberg-slammed-for-puerto-rico-vr-video.html.

Kim, Jooho, and Makarand Hastak. "Social Network Analysis: Characteristics of Online Social Networks after a Disaster." *International Journal of Information Management*, vol. 38, no. 1, Feb. 2018, pp. 86–96. *ScienceDirect*, https://doi.org/10.1016/j.ijinfomgt.2017.08.003.

Kimball, Miles A. "The Golden Age of Technical Communication." *Journal of Technical Writing and Communication*, vol. 47, no. 3, July 2017, pp. 330–58. *Crossref*, https://doi.org/10.1177/0047281616641927.

King, Lisa, et al., editors. *Survivance, Sovereignty, and Story: Teaching American Indian Rhetorics*. Utah State UP, 2015

Kishore, Nishant, et al. "Mortality in Puerto Rico after Hurricane Maria." *New England Journal of Medicine*, vol. 379, no. 2, pp. 162–70, May 2018. https://doi.org/10.1056/NEJMsa1803972.

Klein, Naomi. *The Battle For Paradise: Puerto Rico Takes on the Disaster Capitalists*. Haymarket Books, 2018.

Klopp, Jackie, et al. "We Must Incorporate Social Justice When Planning for Compound Disasters." *State of the Planet*, 12 May 2021, https://news.climate.columbia.edu/2021/05/12/we-must-incorporate-social-justice-when-planning-for-compound-disasters/.

Koerber, Amy. "Rhetorical Agency, Resistance, and the Disciplinary Rhetorics of Breastfeeding." *Technical Communication Quarterly*, vol. 15, no. 1, Jan. 2006, pp. 87–101. *Crossref*, https://doi.org/10.1207/s15427625tcq1501_7.

Kong, Yeqing. "*Water is a Human Right": Exploring Environmental and Public Health Risk Communication in the Flint Water Crisis*. 2021. North Carolina State U, PhD Dissertation.

Kynard, Carmen. "'All I Need Is One Mic': A Black Feminist Community Meditation on the Work, the Job, and the Hustle (& Why So Many of Yall Confuse This Stuff)." *Community Literacy Journal*, vol. 14, no. 2, 2 Oct. 2020. https://doi.org/10.25148/14.2.009033/.

Latour, Bruno. *Reassembling the Social: An Introduction to Actor-Network-Theory*. Oxford UP, 2005.

Lee, Soyeon. "Language Minorities' Localization in COVID-19 Recovery: An Ecological Approach to Navigating Community-Based User Experience." *The 39th ACM International Conference on Design of Communication*, Association for Computing Machinery, 2021, pp. 183–89. *ACM Digital Library*, https://doi.org/10.1145/3472714.3473640.

Leurs, Koen. "The Politics of Transnational Affective Capital: Digital Connectivity among Young Somalis Stranded in Ethiopia." *Crossings: Journal of Migration & Culture*, vol. 5, no. 1, Mar. 2014, pp. 87–104. *EBSCOhost*, https://doi.org/10.1386/cjmc.5.1.87_1.

Lloréns, Hilda. "Imaging Disaster: Puerto Rico through the Eye of Hurricane María." *Transforming Anthropology*, vol. 26, no. 2, 2018, pp. 136–56. *Wiley Online Library*, https://doi.org/10.1111/traa.12126.

Lloréns, Hilda, and Ruth Santiago. "Women Lead Puerto Rico's Recovery." *NACLA Report on the Americas*, vol. 50, no. 4, Dec. 2018, pp. 398–403. *EBSCOhost*, https://doi.org/10.1080/10714839.2018.1550985.

Lloyd, Keith. "Learning from India's *Nyāya* Rhetoric: Debating Analogically through *Vāda*'s Fruitful Dialogue." *Rhetoric Society Quarterly*, vol. 43, no. 3, May 2013, pp. 285–99. *Crossref*, https://doi.org/10.1080/02773945.2013.792698.

Mao, LuMing. "Doing Comparative Rhetoric Responsibly." *Rhetoric Society Quarterly*, vol. 41, no. 1, Jan. 2011, pp. 64–69. *Taylor and Francis+NEJM*, https://doi.org/10.1080/02773945.2010.533149.

Mao, LuMing, et al. "Manifesting a Future for Comparative Rhetoric." *Rhetoric Review*, vol. 34, no. 3, July 2015, pp. 239–74. *Taylor and Francis+NEJM*, https://doi.org/10.1080/07350198.2015.1040105.

Marcus, George E., and Erkan Saka. "Assemblage." *Theory, Culture &*

*Society*, vol. 23, no. 2–3, May 2006, pp. 101–06. *SAGE Journals*, https://doi.org/10.1177/0263276406062573.

Martinez, Aja Y. *Counterstory: The Rhetoric and Writing of Critical Race Theory.* National Council of Teachers of English, 2020.

Massumi, Brian. Foreword. "Translator's Foreword: Pleasures of Philosophy." *A Thousand Plateaus Caplitalism and Schizophrenia* by Gilles Deleuze and Félix Guattari, U of Minnesota P, 1987, pp. ix-xvi

Milken Institute School of Public Health. (2016). Ascertainment of the estimated excess mortality from Hurricane Maria in Puerto Rico. George Washington University. https://tinyurl.com/yhnpjxs4.

Miller, Carolyn R. "A Humanistic Rationale for Technical Writing." *College English*, vol. 40, no. 6, 1979, pp. 610–17. *JSTOR*, https://doi.org/10.2307/375964.

Moffit, J. (2017, June). Choosing a Historical API. *Gnip.* https://support.gnip.com/articles/choosing-historical-api.html.

Moore, Kristen R. "The Technical Communicator as Participant, Facilitator, and Designer in Public Engagement Projects." *Technical Communication*, vol. 64, no. 3, 2017, p. 17.

Murthy, Dhiraj, and Alexander J. Gross. "Social Media Processes in Disasters: Implications of Emergent Technology Use." *Social Science Research*, vol. 63, Mar. 2017, pp. 356–70. *ScienceDirect*, https://doi.org/10.1016/j.ssresearch.2016.09.015.

"Nepal: End Discrimination in Earthquake Relief Effort." *Amnesty International*, 1 June 2015, https://www.amnesty.org/en/latest/news/2015/06/nepal-end-discrimination-in-earthquake-relief-effort/.

Nepal Flash Appeal for Response to the Nepal Earthquake (April-July 2015). United Nations Office for the Coordination of Humanitarian Affairs and Office of the Humanitarian Coordinator and Humanitarian Partners. URL: https://www.undp.org/publications/un-nepal-earthquake-flash-appeal.

"#Nepalquake: List of Food/Shelter/Resources in Affected Areas - [ARCHIVED]." Google Docs curated by Code for Nepal, https://docs.google.com/document/d/1_wLkYkBj1gFUQzpZOvNQQo10AS0vDDOLJ9k-1M1eqQ3M/edit?usp=embed_facebook. Accessed 19 Mar. 2024.

Ortiz Torres, Blanca. "Decoloniality and Community-Psychology Practice in Puerto Rico: Autonomous Organising ( *Autogestión* ) and Self-Determination." *International Review of Psychiatry*, vol. 32, no. 4, May 2020, pp. 359–64. *Crossref*, https://doi.org/10.1080/09540261.2020.1761776.

Papacharissi, Zizi. *Affective Publics: Sentiment, Technology, and Politics*. Oxford UP, 2015.

Parks, Stephen J., and Ahmed Abdelhakim Hachelaf. "Of Rights Without Guarantees: Friction at the Borders of Nations, Digital Spaces, and Classrooms." *Literacy in Composition Studies*, vol. 7, no. 1, 2019, pp.

90–113.

Patil, Vrushali, and Bandana Purkayastha. "The Transnational Assemblage of Indian Rape Culture." *Ethnic and Racial Studies*, vol. 41, no. 11, Sept. 2018, pp. 1952–70. https://doi.org/10.1080/01419870.2017.1322707.

Paudel, Dinesh, and Gregory Reck. *The Global Geopolitics of Disaster: The Case of the Nepali Floods*. Common Dreams, 2017.

Payne, Arwa Damon, Ed. "Nepal Earthquake: Mountain Villages Are Cut off from Almost Everything." *CNN*, 1 May 2015, https://www.cnn.com/2015/05/01/asia/nepal-earthquake/index.html.

Petrun Sayers, Elizabeth L., et al. "'We Will Rise No Matter What': Community Perspectives of Disaster Resilience Following Hurricanes Irma and Maria in Puerto Rico." *Journal of Applied Communication Research*, vol. 51, no. 2, Mar. 2023, pp. 126–45. https://doi.org/10.1080/00909882.2022.2069473.

Pigg, Stacey. "Coordinating Constant Invention: Social Media's Role in Distributed Work." *Technical Communication Quarterly*, vol. 23, no. 2, Apr. 2014, pp. 69–87. *Crossref*, https://doi.org/10.1080/10572252.2013.796545.

Potts, Liza. "Designing for Disaster: Social Software Use in Times of Crisis." *International Journal of Sociotechnology and Knowledge Development*, vol. 1, no. 2, 2009, pp. 33–46. https://doi.org/10.4018/jskd.2009040104.

---. *Social Media in Disaster Response: How Experience Architects Can Build for Participation*. Routledge, 2014.

Potts, Liza, et al. "Tweeting Disaster: Hashtag Constructions and Collisions." *Proceedings of the 29th ACM International Conference on Design of Communication*, Association for Computing Machinery, 2011, pp. 235–40. *ACM Digital Library*, https://doi.org/10.1145/2038476.2038522.

Powell, Katrina M. Identity and Power in Narratives of Displacement. Routledge, 2015.

Powell, Malea. "Rhetorics of Survivance: How American Indians Use Writing." *College Composition and Communication*, vol. 53, no. 3, 2002, pp. 396–434. *JSTOR*, https://doi.org/10.2307/1512132.

*Puerto Rico - History and Heritage | Travel| Smithsonian Magazine*. https://www.smithsonianmag.com/travel/puerto-rico-history-and-heritage-13990189/. Accessed 18 Mar. 2024.

Quijano, Aníbal. "Coloniality and Modernity/Rationality." *Cultural Studies*, vol. 21, no. 2–3, Mar. 2007, pp. 168–78. *Crossref*, https://doi.org/10.1080/09502380601164353.

Regional Overview: Impact of Hurricanes Irma and Maria: Conference Supporting Document. URL: https://reliefweb.int/report/dominica/regional-overview-impact-hurricanes-irma-and-maria.

Reyes Curz, Mariolga. "For Whom We Wait—80grados+." 80grados+

Prensasinprisa, 2 Feb. 2018, https://www.80grados.net/por-quienes-esperamos/.

Rice, Jenny. *Distant Publics: Development Rhetoric and the Subject of Crisis*. U of Pittsburgh P, 2012.

Rice, Jenny Edbauer. "The New 'New': Making a Case for Critical Affect Studies." *Quarterly Journal of Speech*, vol. 94, no. 2, May 2008, pp. 200–12. https://doi.org/10.1080/00335630801975434.

Richards, D. P. "The Challenges of Exploring Local Place as a Context of Use in the Study of Interactive Risk Visualizations: Experience Report." *SIGDOC '17: Proceedings of the 35th ACM International Conference on the Design of Communication*, Association for Computing Machinery, 2017, pp. 1–7. *ACM Digital Library*, https://doi.org/10.1145/3121113.3121208.

Rickert, Thomas J. *Ambient Rhetoric: The Attunements of Rhetorical Being*. U of Pittsburgh P, 2013.

Rodríguez-Díaz, Carlos E. "Maria in Puerto Rico: Natural Disaster in a Colonial Archipelago." *American Journal of Public Health*, vol. 108, no. 1, Jan. 2018, pp. 30–32. *PubMed Central*, https://doi.org/10.2105/AJPH.2017.304198.

Rose, Emma J., et al. "Community-Based User Experience: Evaluating the Usability of Health Insurance Information with Immigrant Patients." *IEEE Transactions on Professional Communication*, vol. 60, no. 2, June 2017, pp. 214–31. *IEEE Xplore*, https://doi.org/10.1109/TPC.2017.2656698.

Royster, Jacqueline Jones. "When the First Voice You Hear Is Not Your Own." *College Composition and Communication*, vol. 47, no. 1, 1996, pp. 29–40. *JSTOR*, https://doi.org/10.2307/358272.

Sackey, Donnie Johnson. "An Environmental Justice Paradigm for Technical Communication. "In *Key Theoretical Frameworks*, edited by Angela M. Haas and Michelle F. Eble, Utah State UP, 2018, pp. 138–60. *JSTOR*, http://www.jstor.org/stable/j.ctv7tq4mx.12.

Sanchez, Nikki. "Decolonization Is for Everyone | Nikki Sanchez | TEDxSFU." Youtube, uploaded by TEDx Talks, 12 Mar. 2019, https://www.youtube.com/watch?v=QP9x1NnCWNY.

Sano-Franchini. "Designing Outrage, Programming Discord: A Critical Interface Analysis of Facebook as a Campaign Technology." *Technical Communication*, vol. 65, no. 4, Nov. 2018, pp. 387–410.

Sapkota, Chandan. *Final Take on Economic and Poverty Impact of Nepal Earthquake*. Asian Development Bank, 2015. https://blogs.adb.org/blog/final-take-economic-and-poverty-impact-nepal-earthquake.

Sauer, Beverly A. *The Rhetoric of Risk: Technical Documentation in Hazardous Environments*. Lawrence Erlbaum Associates, 2003.

Schell, Eileen E. "Transnational Environmental Justice Rhetorics and the Green Belt Movement: Wangari Muta Maathai's Ecological Rhetorics and Literacies." *Journal of Advanced Composition*, vol. 33, no. 3/4, 2013, pp. 585–613. *JSTOR*, http://www.jstor.org/stable/43854569.

Schwarz, Andreas, et al. "Significance and Structure of International Risk and Crisis Communication Research." *The Handbook of International Crisis Communication Research*, John Wiley & Sons, Ltd, 2016, pp. 1–10. *Wiley Online Library*, https://doi.org/10.1002/9781118516812.ch1.

Scott, John, and Peter J. Carrington. *The SAGE Handbook of Social Network Analysis*. SAGE Publications, 2011.

Simmons, W. Michele. *Participation and Power: Civic Discourse in Environmental Policy Decisions*. State U of New York P, 2007.

Sinha, Shreeya. "3 Ways Nepalis Are Using Crowdsourcing to Aid in Quake Relief - The New York Times." *The NewYork Times*, 2015, https://www.nytimes.com/2015/05/02/world/asia/3-ways-nepalis-are-using-crowdsourcing-to-aid-in-quake-relief.html.

Slack, Jennifer Daryl, and J. Macgregor Wise. *Culture and Technology: A Primer*. Peter Lang Publishing, Inc., 2005.

Solon, O. (2017, October). Mark Zuckerberg 'tours' flooded Puerto Rico in bizarre virtual reality promo. *The Guardian*. https://www.theguardian.com/technology/2017/oct/09/mark-zuckerberg-facebook-puerto-rico-virtual-reality.

Soto Vega, Karrieann. "Colonial Causes and Consequences: Climate Change and Climate Chaos in Puerto Rico." *Enculturation*, no. 32, 2020, http://enculturation.net/colonial_causes_consequences.

---. "Puerto Rico Weathers the Storm: Autogestión as a Coalitional Counter-Praxis of Survival." *Feral Feminisms*, no. 9, 2019, p. 17.

Subba, Rajib. "Earthquake Rescue: Twitter for Crisis Communication." *My Republica*, 2015, http://freedomforum.org.np/twitter-for-crisis-communication/.

Subba, Rajib, and Tung Bui. "Online Convergence Behavior, Social Media Communications and Crisis Response: An Empirical Study of the 2015 Nepal Earthquake Police Twitter Project." *Proceedings of the 50th Hawaii International Conference on System Sciences* | 2017, pp. 284–93.

Sullivan, Patricia, and James E Porter. *Opening Spaces: Writing Technologies and Critical Research Practices*. Ablex Pub. Corp, 1997.

Talbot, Jessica, et al. "Informality in Postdisaster Reconstruction: The Role of Social Capital in Reconstruction Management in Post–Hurricane Maria Puerto Rico." *Journal of Management in Engineering*, vol. 36, no. 6, Nov. 2020, p. 04020074. *ASCE*, https://doi.org/10.1061/(ASCE)ME.1943-5479.0000833.

Toya, Hideki, and Mark Skidmore. "Information/Communication Technology and Natural Disaster Vulnerability." *Economics Letters*, vol. 137, Dec. 2015, pp. 143–45. *Crossref*, https://doi.org/10.1016/j.econlet.2015.10.018.

Tuck, Eve, and K. Wayne Yang. "Unbecoming Claims: Pedagogies of Refusal in Qualitative Research." *Qualitative Inquiry*, vol. 20, no. 6, July 2014, pp. 811–18. *Crossref*, https://doi.org/10.1177/1077800414530265.

Walaski, Pamela. "General Concepts of Risk and Crisis Communications." *Risk and Crisis Communications*, John Wiley & Sons, Ltd, 2011, pp. 5–18. https://doi.org/10.1002/9781118093429.ch2.

Walton, Rebecca, et al. *Technical Communication after the Social Justice Turn: Building Coalitions for Action*. Routledge, 2019. *Crossref*, https://doi.org/10.4324/9780429198748.

Walwema, Josephine. "The WHO Health Alert: Communicating a Global Pandemic with WhatsApp." *Journal of Business and Technical Communication*, vol. 35, no. 1, Jan. 2021, pp. 35–40. *SAGE Journals*, https://doi.org/10.1177/1050651920958507.

Wang, Bo. "Comparative Rhetoric, Postcolonial Studies, and Transnational Feminisms: A Geopolitical Approach." *Rhetoric Society Quarterly*, vol. 43, no. 3, May 2013, pp. 226–42. *Crossref*, https://doi.org/10.1080/02773945.2013.792692.

Wang, Zhaozhe. "Activist Rhetoric in Transnational Cyber-Public Spaces: Toward a Comparative Materialist Approach." *Rhetoric Society Quarterly*, vol. 50, no. 4, Aug. 2020, pp. 240–53. *Crossref*, https://doi.org/10.1080/02773945.2020.1748218.

Wasserman, Stanley, and Katherine Faust. *Social Network Analysis: Methods and Applications*. Cambridge UP, 1994.

Watkins, Daphne C., and Deborah Gioia. "First Floor": An Introduction to a "Mixed" Way of Thinking - Oxford Scholarship. https://doi.org/10.1093/acprof:oso/9780199747450.003.0001. Accessed 26 July 2019.

Welhausen, Candice A. *Visualizing a Non-Pandemic: Considerations for Communicating Public Health Risks in Intercultural Contexts*. p. 14.

"WFP to Destroy 7.8 Metric Ton Rotten Rice in Gorkha." *The Himala*yan Times, 20 July 2015, https://thehimalayantimes.com/nepal/wfp-to-destroy-7-8-metric-ton-rotten-rice-in-gorkha.

"Why Is Indian Media Facing a Backlash in Nepal?" *BBC News*, 4 May 2015. https://www.bbc.com/news/world-asia-india-32579561.

Willison, Charley E., et al. "Quantifying Inequities in US Federal Response to Hurricane Disaster in Texas and Florida Compared with Puerto Rico." *BMJ Global Health*, vol. 4, no. 1, Jan. 2019, p. e001191. *gh.bmj.com*, https://doi.org/10.1136/bmjgh-2018-001191.

Yam, Shui-yin Sharon. "Affective Economies and Alienizing Discourse: Citizenship and Maternity Tourism in Hong Kong." Rhetoric Society Quarterly, vol. 46, no. 5, Oct. 2016, pp. 410–33. https://doi.org/10.1080/02773945.2016.1159721.

Zorrilla, Carmen. "The View from Puerto Rico—Hurricane Maria and Its Aftermath." *The New England Journal of Medicine*, vol. 377, no. 19,

2017, https://doi.org/10.1056/NEJMp1713196.
Zukerberg, M. (2015, April). Activation of safety check feature on Facebook [Facebook update]. https://www.facebook.com/photo.php?fbid=10102060884238261&set=a.612287952871&type=1&theater

# Index

## Author

Photo by Leslie King

**Sweta Baniya**, originally from Nepal, is an assistant professor of rhetoric and professional and technical writing and an affiliate faculty of Women and Gender Studies at Virginia Polytechnic Institute and State University. Through a transnational and non-Western perspective, her research focuses on transnational coalitions in disaster response, crisis communication, non-Western rhetoric, and transnational feminism. Her dissertation received the 2021 CCCC Outstanding Dissertation Award in Technical Communication-Honorable Mention. She is also the recipient of the CCCC Chairs' Memorial Scholarship (2020), CCCC Scholars for the Dream Award (2019), CPTSC and Bedford/St. Martin's Diversity Scholarship Award (2019), ATTW Amplification Award (2019), and Kairos Service Award for Graduate Students and Adjuncts (2019), among others. Dr. Baniya's scholarship has appeared in *Technical Communication Quarterly, Technical Communication, Enculturation, Journal of Business & Technical Communication, Community Literacy Journal, IEEE Transactions on Professional Communication, Programmatic Perspective,* and *Journal of Technological Studies*, among others. Dr. Baniya's research and collaborative community work has been funded via Digital Justice Seed Grant by the American Council of Learned Societies, 4-VA Initiative, USAID, SIGDOC's Career Advancement Grant, CCCC's Research Initiative, among others. She teaches both graduate and undergraduate courses at Virginia Tech that focus on rhetorics in the global society, global community engagement, intercultural communication, user documentation, and disaster /crisis communication. Prior to pursuing her PhD, she worked as English News Reader and Editor at Nepal's national radio, Radio Nepal, for eight years as well as worked as a journalist for the Nepal Bureau of Xinhua News Agency. Similarly, she also worked as Communications Officer for United Nations Human Settlements Program (UN-Habitat) in Nepal, Teach for Nepal, and DanChurch Aid. Her research and teaching blends her multitude of professional experiences.

# BOOKS IN THE CCCC STUDIES IN WRITING & RHETORIC SERIES

*Transnational Assemblages: Social Justice and Crisis Communication during Disaster*
Sweta Baniya

*Memoria: Essays in Honor of Victor Villanueva*
Edited by Asao B. Inoue, Wendy Olson, and Siskanna Naynaha

*The Hands of God at Work: Islamic Gender Justice through Translingual Praxis*
Amber Engelson

*Queer Techné: Bodies, Rhetorics, and Desire in the History of Computing*
Patricia Fancher

*Living English, Moving Literacies: Women's Stories of Learning between the US and Nepal*
Katie Silvester

*Recollections from an Uncommon Time 4C20 Documentarian Tales*
Edited by Julie Lindquist, Bree Straayer, and Bump Halbritter

*Teachers Talking Writing: Perspectives on Places, Pedagogies, and Programs*
Shane A. Wood

*Materiality and Writing Studies: Aligning Labor, Scholarship, and Teaching*
Holly Hassel and Cassandra Phillips

*Rhetorics of Overcoming: Rewriting Narratives of Disability and Accessibility in Writing Studies*
Allison Harper Hitt

*Writing Accomplices with Student Immigrant Rights Organizers*
Glenn Hutchinson

*Counterstory: The Rhetoric and Writing of Critical Race Theory*
Aja Y. Martinez

*Writing Programs, Veterans Studies, and the Post-9/11 University: A Field Guide*
Alexis Hart and Roger Thompson

*Beyond Progress in the Prison Classroom: Options and Opportunities*
Anna Plemons

*Rhetorics Elsewhere and Otherwise: Contested Modernities, Decolonial Visions*
Edited by Romeo García & Damián Baca

*Black Perspectives in Writing Program Administration: From the Margins to the Center*
Edited by Staci M. Perryman-Clark and Collin Lamont Craig

*Translanguaging outside the Academy: Negotiating Rhetoric and Healthcare in the Spanish Caribbean*
Rachel Bloom-Pojar

*Collaborative Learning as Democratic Practice: A History*
Mara Holt

*Reframing the Relational: A Pedagogical Ethic for Cross-Curricular Literacy Work*
Sandra L. Tarabochia

*Inside the Subject: A Theory of Identity for the Study of Writing*
Raúl Sánchez

*Genre of Power: Police Report Writers and Readers in the Justice System*
Lcslic Sc0p3.5awright

*Assembling Composition*
Edited by Kathleen Blake Yancey and Stephen J. McElroy

*Public Pedagogy in Composition Studies*
Ashley J. Holmes

*From Boys to Men: Rhetorics of Emergent American Masculinity*
Leigh Ann Jones

*Freedom Writing: African American Civil Rights Literacy Activism, 1955–1967*
Rhea Estelle Lathan

*The Desire for Literacy: Writing in the Lives of Adult Learners*
Lauren Rosenberg

*On Multimodality: New Media in Composition Studies*
Jonathan Alexander and Jacqueline Rhodes

*Toward a New Rhetoric of Difference*
Stephanie L. Kerschbaum

*Rhetoric of Respect: Recognizing Change at a Community Writing Center*
Tiffany Rousculp

*After Pedagogy: The Experience of Teaching*
Paul Lynch

*Redesigning Composition for Multilingual Realities*
Jay Jordan

*Agency in the Age of Peer Production*
Quentin D. Vieregge, Kyle D. Stedman, Taylor Joy Mitchell, & Joseph M. Moxley

*Remixing Composition: A History of Multimodal Writing Pedagogy*
Jason Palmeri

*First Semester: Graduate Students, Teaching Writing, and the Challenge of Middle Ground*
Jessica Restaino

*Agents of Integration: Understanding Transfer as a Rhetorical Act*
Rebecca S. Nowacek

*Digital Griots: African American Rhetoric in a Multimedia Age*
Adam J. Banks

*The Managerial Unconscious in the History of Composition Studies*
Donna Strickland

*Everyday Genres: Writing Assignments across the Disciplines*
Mary Soliday

*The Community College Writer: Exceeding Expectations*
Howard Tinberg and Jean-Paul Nadeau

*A Taste for Language: Literacy, Class, and English Studies*
James Ray Watkins

*Before Shaughnessy: Basic Writing at Yale and Harvard, 1920–1960*
Kelly Ritter

*Writer's Block: The Cognitive Dimension*
Mike Rose

*Teaching/Writing in Thirdspaces: The Studio Approach*
Rhonda C. Grego and Nancy S. Thompson

*Rural Literacies*
Kim Donehower, Charlotte Hogg, and Eileen E. Schell

*Writing with Authority: Students' Roles as Writers in Cross-National Perspective*
David Foster

*Whistlin' and Crowin' Women of Appalachia: Literacy Practices since College*
Katherine Kelleher Sohn

*Sexuality and the Politics of Ethos in the Writing Classroom*
Zan Meyer Gonçalves

*African American Literacies Unleashed: Vernacular English and the Composition Classroom*
Arnetha F. Ball and Ted Lardner

*Revisionary Rhetoric, Feminist Pedagogy, and Multigenre Texts*
Julie Jung

*Archives of Instruction: Nineteenth-Century Rhetorics, Readers, and Composition Books in the United States*
Jean Ferguson Carr, Stephen L. Carr, and Lucille M. Schultz

*Response to Reform: Composition and the Professionalization of Teaching*
Margaret J. Marshall

*Multiliteracies for a Digital Age*
Stuart A. Selber

*Personally Speaking: Experience as Evidence in Academic Discourse*
Candace Spigelman

*Self-Development and College Writing*
Nick Tingle

*Minor Re/Visions: Asian American Literacy Narratives as a Rhetoric of Citizenship*
Morris Young

*A Communion of Friendship: Literacy, Spiritual Practice, and Women in Recovery*
Beth Daniell

*Embodied Literacies: Imageword and a Poetics of Teaching*
Kristie S. Fleckenstein

*Language Diversity in the Classroom: From Intention to Practice*
Edited by Geneva Smitherman and Victor Villanueva

*Rehearsing New Roles: How College Students Develop as Writers*
Lee Ann Carroll

*Across Property Lines: Textual Ownership in Writing Groups*
Candace Spigelman

*Mutuality in the Rhetoric and Composition Classroom*
David L. Wallace and Helen Rothschild Ewald

*The Young Composers: Composition's Beginnings in Nineteenth-Century Schools*
Lucille M. Schultz

*Technology and Literacy in the Twenty-First Century: The Importance of Paying Attention*
Cynthia L. Selfe

*Women Writing the Academy: Audience, Authority, and Transformation*
Gesa E. Kirsch

*Gender Influences: Reading Student Texts*
Donnalee Rubin

*Something Old, Something New: College Writing Teachers and Classroom Change*
Wendy Bishop

*Dialogue, Dialectic, and Conversation: A Social Perspective on the Function of Writing*
Gregory Clark

*Audience Expectations and Teacher Demands*
Robert Brooke and John Hendricks

*Toward a Grammar of Passages*
Richard M. Coe

*Rhetoric and Reality: Writing Instruction in American Colleges, 1900–1985*
James A. Berlin

*Writing Groups: History, Theory, and Implications*
Anne Ruggles Gere

*Teaching Writing as a Second Language*
Alice S. Horning

*Invention as a Social Act*
Karen Burke LeFevre

*The Variables of Composition: Process and Product in a Business Setting*
Glenn J. Broadhead and Richard C. Freed

*Writing Instruction in Nineteenth-Century American Colleges*
James A. Berlin

*Computers & Composing: How the New Technologies Are Changing Writing*
Jeanne W. Halpern and Sarah Liggett

*A New Perspective on Cohesion in Expository Paragraphs*
Robin Bell Markels

*Evaluating College Writing Programs*
Stephen P. Witte and Lester Faigley

This book was typeset in Garamond and Frutiger by Mike Palmquist.
Typefaces used on the cover include Garamond and News Gothic.